Made Whole

Made Whole

The Practical Guide to Reaching Your Financial Goals

....

Tiffany Aliche

The Budgetnista

RODALE

NEW YORK

Published in the United States by Rodale Books, an imprint of Random House,
a division of Penguin Random House LLC, New York.
RodaleBooks.com | RandomHouseBooks.com

Rodale Books is a registered trademark, and the Circle colophon is a trademark of
Penguin Random House LLC.

Library of Congress Cataloging-in-Publication Data has been applied for.

ISBN 978-0-593-58129-2
Ebook ISBN 978-0-593-58130-8

Printed in the United States of America

Book design by Andrea Lau
Cover photograph by Tinnetta Bell

1st Printing

First Edition

CONTENTS

Introduction   *1*

CHAPTER 1
The *Made Whole* Map and Mindset   *7*

CHAPTER 2
10% Whole: Build Your Budget   *15*

CHAPTER 3
20% Whole: Save Like a Squirrel   *51*

CHAPTER 4
30% Whole: Dig Out of Debt   *65*

CHAPTER 5
40% Whole: Score High (Credit)   *91*

CHAPTER 6
50% Whole: Learn to Earn (Increase Your Income)   *111*

CHAPTER 7
60% Whole: Invest Like an Insider (Retirement and Wealth)   *129*

CHAPTER 8
70% Whole: Get Good with Insurance   *167*

CHAPTER 9
80% Whole: Grow Rich*ish* (Increase Your Net Worth)   *201*

CHAPTER 10
90% Whole: Pick Your Money Team (Financial Professionals)   *213*

CHAPTER 11
100% Whole: Leave a Legacy (Estate Planning)   *231*

Made Whole

INTRODUCTION

In 2021, I published a book called *Get Good with Money*, aka *GGWM*. I wrote it to help people pursue and achieve financial wholeness, which is the state a person has achieved when the ten fundamental areas of their financial life are in working order and they have a realistic picture of the path they need to be on to reach their dreams. The response to the book was beyond what I could have ever imagined. Hundreds of thousands of people (and counting!) latched on to the *GGWM* blueprint, using it to build a solid foundation for their financial future.

Since that time, I've seen and heard so many inspirational stories and marveled at the work people are willing to put in to lift themselves up. And I know there are many more people who are ready to level up; all they need is access to the right tools and a teacher to guide them.

As a former preschool teacher and current financial educator, I have found it incredibly rewarding to step in and share the kind of guidance that can make a difference in people's lives. And it's the teacher in me that brought me back to offer you *Made Whole*. I know that sometimes to get *real* work done, you need a place to do it.

And that's what you're going to find in the pages ahead: a space to document your dreams about your financial future, maybe a few screams about your financial past (I get it—I've got plenty of those too), and the details you'll use to complete one fundamental component of financial wholeness at a time.

Meeting You Where You Are

Now let's talk about *you* for a minute. You may have picked up this workbook as a reader of *GGWM*, and if that's the case, I am thrilled to have you back. Or you could be here as a new reader, and to you I say, "Welcome!" In either case, *Made Whole* has so much to offer. To help you get the most out of it, I want to provide some guidance before you dive in.

For readers of *GGWM*: I hope that *Get Good with Money* was good to you, and that the key lesson you took away was that financial wholeness isn't one big untamable beast but instead a collection of ten key components that can be achieved when they're taken on individually. I hope that you established a budget, worked through your debt, boosted your credit score, got strategic about earning, and more. But it's possible you didn't get as far as you would have liked. Maybe life interrupted; maybe you wished that the investing chapter was just a tad bit shorter so you could have made your way all the way through it. *I get it.*

Here's the truth: Even with a compartmentalized approach, managing and maintaining the pursuit of 100% wholeness while also doing the heavy lifting of living your life can be tough. That's why I'm happy you're here with your hands on *Made Whole*. I like to think of this workbook as the perfect companion to *Get Good with Money*; it's a little bit like the CliffsNotes version of it, with the bonus of allowing you to write and do your work directly in the book. Or put it this way: It's a little bit like the concentrated juice version of it, but instead of water, you just add work to get the full goodness.

For new readers: I am so excited that you are here and about to start a journey that could have a profound impact on your life. When you focus on the components of financial wholeness, you set yourself (and even your descendants) up to achieve the ultimate goal of peace of mind around money.

Since you're new, you might be wondering why it is exactly that you should take my advice. And I appreciate that curiosity because I would be wondering the same thing. Trust is something that has to be earned, and I'm basically asking you to trust what I tell you to do in one of the most important areas of your life. So, let me give you a little background.

My name is Tiffany Aliche. I was born on October 16 . . . OK, just kidding. I'm not going to go that far back. But I will tell you that I'm a first-generation Nigerian American. My parents were both born and raised in small, rural villages in Nigeria and came to the United States for education and opportunity. They earned two degrees each and had successful careers as a chief financial officer (my dad) and a registered nurse (my mom). They did all this while raising me and my four amazing sisters. We've always been a super-close family, and family is my priority in life. (Although travel is a close second!)

My parents, and especially my dad, raised us to be very financially aware; there were always financial lessons being taught in our home. It's not like he had us tapping away at a calculator each day or staring at a chalkboard full of numbers; he just had a way of teaching financial awareness through real-life experiences. I didn't realize it at the time, but this definitely informed my later interest in becoming an educator and my own style of teaching.

These lessons helped set me up to be smart with my money from a young age. By the time I was twenty-six, I owned a condo and had $40,000 saved. All on a $39,000-a-year teacher's salary, plus a few side hustles like tutoring. Yet I was almost too smart for my own good, and my overconfidence led me to make some big mistakes. The kind of mistakes that would take everything I had made away from me and leave me, at age thirty, unemployed (my job was eliminated during the 2008 recession), living with my parents (my condo was foreclosed on), and with no savings to speak of (due to some poor investment choices and a scammer). I was at a lifetime low.

It was my good friend Linda who would pick me up out of the ashes. She provided a kind and nonjudgmental ear. She helped me forgive myself for my mistakes and let go of the shame I felt so I could start to rebuild my life. I had all the skills; I just had to remember them. I'd been taught how to budget, how to save, how to get out of debt, how to manage my credit. It was time to revisit all those invaluable lessons I'd been taught growing up. As I returned to them, I began to write them down.

I became really focused on fixing my financial situation and lifting myself back up—and my friends noticed. They too had experienced financial distress as a result of the recession. "Can you help me too?" many of them started to ask. And so I began giving lessons every weekend and helping friends create plans to improve their financial health. My little sister, Lisa, started calling me The Budgetnista.

Before I knew it, this humble side hustle started to grow into something bigger. I spent an increasing amount of time helping people with different financial challenges and creating solutions for and with them. After a couple of years of volunteering my financial coaching services, I was invited by my local United Way to teach a series of financial classes to the community. And in that moment, my business identity was born. I became The Budgetnista, financial educator. My mission: to help empower people to better their lives by focusing on financial health.

I couldn't believe how popular the classes were. There was interest only locally at first, but then I started to get requests from people out of state, and then from out of the country. They wanted to know where they could access the classes. So I got to work on converting all the lessons into an online curriculum that I would call the Live Richer Challenge, or LRC (lipericherchallenge.com).

Once I had the LRC curriculum established, I created a goal for myself to get ten thousand women to sign up for the challenge. I began promoting it online, and through word of mouth and social media, I hit my goal!

After the first year of the LRC, I had an incredible twenty thousand additional women sign on to let me help them. I was so inspired and excited! And the results and response were so amazing that I began hosting Live Richer Challenges every year. Since the original ten thousand women were a foundational part of helping me help others pursue their dreams, I dubbed them my Dream Catchers. This name would go on to describe an entire community that is now more than two million strong!

This community has continually helped me elevate my aspirations, just as it has for so many other people. Together we've dreamed big, and I honestly wouldn't be where I am today without them. I got *Get Good with Money* out into the world with their support, and now I'm here sharing *Made Whole* with you (and them, too, of course!).

Now that you know a little more about me, let's get back to you and how to use this book.

How to Use This Book

In the pages ahead, you will find one chapter dedicated to each component of financial wholeness. And within each chapter, you will find the following sections: The Plan, What You'll Need, Do the Work, and The Review.

The Plan will outline the overall goal of the chapter and provide you with the steps that will help you approach and achieve this goal.

What You'll Need is pretty self-explanatory, but make sure you review this section as it will help you gather any information, tools, or additional resources you might need as you work through the chapter.

Do the Work will walk you through the specific action steps you need to complete to make progress toward achieving the objective of the chapter. This will often be the area where you'll need to grab a pen or pencil and get to work.

The Review is a quick and simple review of what you just completed. If you see anything here that doesn't sound familiar, you may want to jump back into the chapter to see what you missed!

In some but not all the chapters, you will find a **Quick Start** section. This will introduce you to an action you can take to get some financial momentum going before you even complete the chapter. These are optional, and if you choose to complete the Quick Start, you'll want to also make sure to complete the rest of the chapter.

I've also created something that I call the *Made Whole* tool kit, which is where you'll be able to easily access resources I've shared throughout the book. This free, downloadable tool kit will include websites I've mentioned, worksheets, spreadsheets, and quizzes. You can access the it at madewholeworkbook.com.

I'm so thrilled you are here, and remember: I am only a social media shout-out away should you ever want to share or seek help. I am @thebudgetnista everywhere!

CHAPTER 1

The *Made Whole* Map and Mindset

Think of financial wholeness as a destination—a "place" to set your sights on and focus your energy toward. With this mindset, you will have "wins" all along the way, and even the small steps of progress you make as you pursue becoming 100% whole can be life-changing. After all, success is like the layers of a cake. Each good choice builds on the one before it. And before you know it, all the seemingly small choices and adjustments you've made come together to create an amazing dessert. The cake you've built holds remarkable power. It represents all your growth as a result of all you've learned.

TIFFANY TIP: At the end of every school year, my dad always reminded me and my sisters that we'd reached a new level of education and that, as he said, "knowledge once given can never be rescinded." That's how it'll be for you as you proceed through the levels of financial wholeness!

To help you get prepared for your journey, I want to give you a preview of the steps to come and share some mindset tools to help you make the most of your good work.

The Ten Steps of Financial Wholeness

The path to financial wholeness has ten steps. Each step—which corresponds to one of the next ten chapters!—is related to an area of your finances, and some will require more work than others.

1. **Build Your Budget:** Learn how to create and semi-automate a personal budget and open the necessary checking and savings accounts to support your budget.
2. **Save Like a Squirrel:** Calculate the savings goal number needed to meet at least three months' worth of expenses for your household. Then calculate how much you need to save each week and month to achieve this goal within twelve to eighteen months.
3. **Dig Out of Debt:** Write out your total debt, payments, and interest rates using the My Debt List template at madewholeworkbook.com; this will give you a clear picture of what you owe. Then choose a debt-repayment strategy and formulate your payoff plan.
4. **Score High (Credit):** Pull your credit score to see where you stand. Make a list of the factors that are impacting your score, then come up with a game plan to improve it.
5. **Learn to Earn (Increase Your Income):** List all the things you've accomplished at your job in the last few years that make a good argument for you to get a raise. Then make a list of all the tasks or jobs you do at work so you can uncover your side-hustle skills. Develop an action plan that lists what you'll do next to increase your income.
6. **Invest Like an Insider:** Use automated investment plans for retirement and wealth building. Speak with HR about retirement plans or set up your

own retirement account(s). Automate an amount to go into retirement and brokerage accounts and increase contributions as your income increases.

7. **Get Good with Insurance:** Make sure you have proper insurance coverage. That means understanding and calculating your needs around life, disability, auto, and home insurance and more.

8. **Get Rich*ish* (Increase Your Net Worth):** Learn how to calculate your net worth and how to achieve and maintain a positive net worth. Create a net worth goal, and define actions you're going to take each month to achieve it.

9. **Pick Your Money Team:** Choose an accountability partner, and find yourself reliable and trustworthy financial professionals.

10. **Leave a Legacy (Estate Planning):** Actively plan for what will happen to your estate (cash, real estate, jewelry, and other assets) after you die. This is important no matter the size of your bank account and portfolio.

I know that at first glance it might seem like a lot to take on. And I want to be real with you—*it is.* But with patience and dedication, it can be done. And it will be made easier if you take advantage of the opportunity to answer questions and complete the exercises throughout the book; these are designed to help you create a deeper connection to the work, and they will help you track your progress along the way.

Financial Wholeness at a Glance

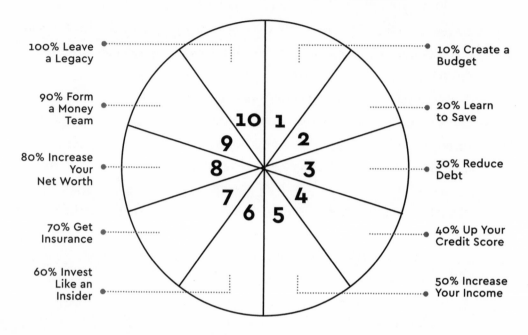

100% Leave a Legacy

90% Form a Money Team

80% Increase Your Net Worth

70% Get Insurance

60% Invest Like an Insider

10% Create a Budget

20% Learn to Save

30% Reduce Debt

40% Up Your Credit Score

50% Increase Your Income

The *Made Whole* Mindset

There's a lot of financial guidance out there, but too often the emotional element—that is, what it *feels* like to look directly at the most important facets of your financial life—is left out. The problem with this is that *not* addressing your emotions can get in the way of moving forward and making progress. It's so easy to get stuck on the fear or feelings of overwhelm, or the sadness and shame that may come up around the topic of money and your history with it. But you can overcome these obstacles by acknowledging their presence and making some mental plans to work through them.

I've found that there are two mindset prep steps that really help. These work to sort of wipe the slate clean and set you up for the kind of success that sticks.

Step 1: Share Your Shame

Shame thrives in the shadows, and it needs silence to be strong. And the stronger and bigger your shame grows, the more it can hide from you. When you share your shame around financial setbacks you've experienced or poor money decisions you've made, you take away its power. I felt so much shame around the financial mistakes I made that I became almost paralyzed to turn things around. The shame kept me from seeing solutions.

I finally started the process of getting past my shame by giving voice to it. I shared my embarrassing financial situation with the kindest person I know—my best friend, Linda. Telling her about the financial hole I'd fallen into was the start of my journey toward digging my way out.

So, here's my assignment for you: Pick the kindest person you know, and share a financial secret with them. This person might become your accountability partner—aka financial bestie—who helps keep you on track (as you help keep them on track) throughout your journey to financial wholeness. But for now, focus on getting your shame off your shoulders and out of the way.

Repeat (and write) after me: *I will share my shame with someone I know, love, and trust. I will not keep trying to carry this weight all by myself.*

_____

_____

_____

Step 2: Give Yourself Grace and Space

I made some mistakes in my twenties that left me in serious financial distress. Here are some of my financial stats at the time:

- I had $35,000 of credit card debt (due to a scam), $52,000 in student loans, and a $220,000 mortgage.
- My savings was depleted.
- I had recently been laid off from my preschool teaching job.
- I had lost my condo to foreclosure.
- I had to move back in with my parents.

I was essentially the opposite of financially whole! I lacked structure and intention and planning across the board, and I couldn't forgive myself for it all. I know that might sound dramatic, but it's true—it wasn't until I said to myself, *It's OK, Tiffany; you didn't intentionally harm anyone, you made money mistakes,* that I was able to share my shame with Linda and start to forge a new financial path.

When I look back at that time, I realize that I had to give myself grace and space before I could evolve. I needed *grace,* the root of kindness and compassion, and *space,* the room to be simultaneously flawed and capable of flourishing in the future.

As you prepare to embark on your own path toward financial wholeness, I want you to think about your own financial history and any regret or remorse you have about choices you've made or circumstances around which you've tied yourself up in a lot of blame. No matter what your specific scenario, this story is not serving you—it's time to let it go. First, find your own Linda and give voice to your shame. If you don't have someone to share this burden with, talk to me. I'm @thebudgetnista on all platforms, and I'm listening. Once you've cracked open the door, it's time to forgive yourself by saying:

It's OK if I don't know the next step—my future is full of potential.

It's OK if I made a mistake—new opportunities abound.

It's OK if I let myself down—my past doesn't dictate my future.

Whew, is it just me or are your eyes sweating after reading those phrases aloud? Repeat (and write) after me: *No matter what, I will give myself grace and space.*

_____

_____

_____

Creating an Environment of Support

Emotional "housekeeping" is an important part of tending to your personal finances, but your physical housekeeping matters too. Taking the time to set up your environment in a way that makes you feel calm can help reduce stress as you get started on the steps to financial wholeness. Here are some things to add to the spot where you'll keep your financial house in order, whether that's a whole room, a nook, or just a tabletop in your home where you'll sit to do this work:

- A scented candle—one that makes you want to settle in and stay awhile
- An emotional support blanket—you know the one (and you might have to fight your significant other, roomie, or kids for it)
- Fuzzy socks/shoes—I love my fuzzy leopard-print house slippers
- A relaxing personalized playlist—Sade is my favorite
- This workbook!

I would love to hear about any of the additions you make to your space that you find helpful! Share it with me on social and use the hashtag #madewholemadebetter.

CHAPTER 2

10% Whole
Build Your Budget

A budget is the foundation of your financial life, and contrary to what a lot of people think, having one can be freeing, not restricting. In fact, I like to think of a budget as a "Say Yes" plan because it can be used to make your dreams come true.

A lot of people tell me they have a budget. But when I ask if their budget is a ballpark number they try to stick to each month or a formal document—written or typed—that reflects itemized income, expenses, and savings, the response is usually, "Well, um . . . more like the ballpark number."

A vague idea or an estimation of the hard numbers that make up your financial life is a budget with a lowercase *b*, or what I call a "baby budget." If you *think* you make X amount each month but don't *know* the exact number down to the cents, if you *think* you spend Y amount each month but don't *know* where it all goes, well, you've got yourself a baby budget. It's time for your baby budget to grow up!

The good news is that maturing your budget doesn't take any special skill or science; it just takes a little time and effort to get the real numbers documented in one place. I call this place your Money List. Your Money List is a detailed collection of your income and expenses that will provide you with a clear picture of your cash flow (in both directions—Money In and Money Out). This picture will open your eyes to how much money you have each month and how you can best manage it through automation and other simple, smart strategies.

I could say a whole lot more on the topic of budget since I am, well, The Budgetnista. But this is a *workbook*, which means you came to do work, and I want to honor that. However, I will tell you just one more itty-bitty thing: The budgeting steps in this chapter are gold—and they are here to make you shine. When I say they are gold, I mean that they work! They have been refined over the last twenty years and tested by literally millions of people who, like you, are aiming for the freedom that comes with financial wholeness.

The Plan for Budget Building

In this chapter, you will learn how to create and semi-automate (via automated transfers and bill payments, etc.) a personal budget and open the necessary checking and savings accounts to support it. This process requires eight simple steps. Let me break it down:

1. Making a Money-In list
2. Making a Money-Out list
3. Calculating how much each Money-Out expense costs monthly
4. Calculating your beginning savings
5. Assigning control categories to your expenses
6. Reducing your expenses as needed and looking for ways to increase your income, then recalculating!
7. Separating your funds
8. And finally, getting automated

Don't worry, I've got you on all this!

WHAT YOU'LL NEED

✓ Recent bank and credit card statements, plus some receipts that reflect routine or recurring expenses

✓ A cute journal or notebook or your laptop—whichever you want to use for any overflow Money List notes (there's space for notes provided in this book, but you may need more room!)

✓ A candle, a nice cup of tea—something that will bring calming energy to counter any stress you might feel about working on your budget

✓ A commitment to do some work to see some wins

Quick Start: Split It Before You Get It!

Want to get a head start on controlling your spending habits, even before you have a grown-up budget? The fastest way to do that is to split your money before you get it! This means going to your HR department and asking to have your paycheck automatically divided, with specific amounts deposited into four separate accounts so that you don't have to take those steps yourself (and risk forgetting or "forgetting" to do so!). Those four accounts are (1) Bills (a checking account), (2) Spending (a checking account), (3) Emergency Savings (a savings account), and (4) Goal Savings (a savings account). If you are self-employed, you will want to set up auto transfers so that anytime you or a client deposits money into your bank, the percentages you want to go to each account are predecided and automatic. See steps 7 and 8 later in this chapter for more details about where to set these accounts up and how to use them most effectively.

How do you know how much you'll need to put into each of these four accounts? Create your Money List by following the upcoming budgeting steps.

SHAKE OUT YOUR FEARS

If the thought of putting your budget under a microscope makes you want to run and hide, let's shake that out a little. Why does it feel scary to you? What will you accomplish if you keep your budget secret from yourself? What will you accomplish if you roll up your sleeves and do the work to discover where all your money goes? Getting real with your money can liberate you from the stress that the secrets help create. Use the space below to jot down how all this makes you feel—that's the first step to feeling better about it!

_____

_____

_____

_____

_____

_____

_____

_____

_____

_____

_____

_____

_____

_____

_____

Budget Building Step 1: Make a Money-In List

Your Money-In List is an itemization of all forms of income you receive each month. There was a time when income was from one job and you got two, maybe four pay-checks a month and that was it. But life seems to have gotten complicated in the area of income (and just about every other area too!), so many people need a second or third job or at least a side hustle just to make ends meet, let alone get ahead. I mention this so that when you're creating your Money-In List, you make sure to count every penny. If it's coming in, it's going down on the list.

Here are some examples of income:

- Your salary or hourly wage
- Any kind of side-hustle earnings
- Spousal or child support
- Investment interest income
- Government-generated payments (e.g., Social Security, disability, financial aid)

DO THE WORK ·······················➤

I've provided my friend Tamecka's Money-In List below. This example should give you an idea of how yours will look once you've completed the blank version below hers. You can also access a digital Money List template in the *Made Whole* tool kit at madewholeworkbook.com.

Once you have a Money-In List, do the simple addition to come up with a total amount. This number is your Total Monthly Take-Home Pay. Got it? Excellent—you've got yourself a budding budget!

TAMECKA'S MONEY-IN LIST	
TOTAL MONTHLY TAKE-HOME (money in)	
MONEY IN (NAME)	MONEY IN (AMOUNT)
Monthly Salary from Job	$3,200.00
Lyft	$650.00
Etsy Shop	$300.00
TOTAL	$4,150.00

→ *Tamecka's Total Monthly Take-Home Pay*

Now create a Money-In List of your own.

MY MONEY-IN LIST	
TOTAL MONTHLY TAKE-HOME (money in)	
MONEY IN (NAME)	MONEY IN (AMOUNT)
	$
	$
	$
TOTAL	$

Budget Building Step 2: Make a Money-Out List

All right, it's time to talk about the money that goes out . . . out of your wallet, out of your bank account, out into the economy. We'll get to accounting for *how much* is going out in a minute, but to start, I find that it's really helpful to simply list the things you regularly spend money on by name. This step will help give you an overall sense of your spending habits and can establish a more powerful connection to the ins and outs of your cash flow than data on a spreadsheet.

Craft your Money-Out List by thinking of your regular day, then building out to your typical week and month. For example, each day, you might buy coffee and a bagel or a take-out lunch. Each week, gas and groceries, a dinner out, or movie tickets. Each month, you probably have a rent or mortgage payment as well as recurring expenses for the internet, your phone, and insurance (like medical or dental insurance and coverage for your home or auto).

I also want you to think about the things you spend on more broadly. Do you bring clothes in for dry cleaning every week? Do you have a monthly haircut? Or a standing monthly girls' night out?

Money spent on *others* counts too. Daycare, your kids' school clothes, and *their* phone bills. What about birthday gifts for your family members or, if you have kids, for their friends' parties?

Don't forget to consider your digital purchases too—like any time you check your CVV code on a card to confirm an online purchase or use a card in a store. If you still use good old cash to pay for things, make note of those instances too. This is all part of your Money-Out story.

DO THE WORK ·····················➤

Here is Tamecka's Money-Out List template—her expenses might help you think of all the ways *you* spend, and give you ideas as you get to work on your own Money-Out List using the blank spreadsheet on the next page. Remember, right now you are only jotting down descriptive terms for these spending categories. We'll get to the dollar amounts in a minute. Again, you can also access a digital template via the *Made Whole* tool kit online.

TAMECKA'S MONEY-OUT LIST (NAMES)	
MONEY OUT (NAME)	
Mortgage	
Car Note	
Car Insurance	
Student Loan (Federal)	
Cell Phone	
Internet	
Visa	
Mastercard	
Store Credit Card	
Utilities (Water, Gas, Electric)	
Groceries	
Toiletries	
Grooming (Haircut, Eyebrows, Nails)	
Dining Out (Breakfast, Lunch, Dinner)	
Entertainment	

MY MONEY-OUT LIST (NAMES)	
MONEY OUT (NAME)	

Budget Building Step 3: Calculate How Much Each Money-Out Expense Costs Monthly

It's now time to assign dollar amounts to the expenses you described in your Money-Out List and add them up to arrive at your Total Monthly Spending Amount.

For some people, the thought of seeing a real number that represents a spending total can bring up some uncomfortable feelings—and that's OK. It's normal to feel anxious when something unknown is about to become something known. But it's the knowing that's going to help your budget mature and help you make progress toward financial wholeness.

One thing to note—if you went all diva detective in capturing the story of your spending, you may have ended up with a verrry long list of expenses. That's great! But as you go through assigning dollar amounts, you may notice that some of the expenses are very similar, such as coffee, lunches, or dinners out. For the sake of simplicity, you can begin to combine these types of similar expenses, in this case under the heading "Eating Out."

DO THE WORK ·······················➤

Using the next template, begin to add dollar amounts to the expenses you described on your Money-Out List. Again, I've included Tamecka's work to help guide your own. Be sure to keep in mind that the intention is to calculate your total spending for one month. Working with this time frame may require some basic math in some cases. For example, if you pay a utility bill every three months, divide by three to get your monthly expense. Or if you pay for your child's daycare each week, you'll want to multiply this expense by four to come up with the monthly cost.

TAMECKA'S MONEY-OUT LIST (AMOUNTS)	
TOTAL MONTHLY SPENDING (MONEY OUT)	
MONEY OUT (NAME)	**MONEY OUT (AMOUNT)**
Mortgage	$2,600.00
Car Note	$300.00
Car Insurance	$235.00
Student Loan (Federal)	$250.00
Cell Phone	$150.00
Internet	$80.00
Visa	$195.00
Mastercard	$50.00
Store Credit Card	$75.00
Utilities (Water, Gas, Electric)	$300.00
Groceries	$100.00
Toiletries	$100.00
Grooming (Haircut, Eyebrows, Nails)	$75.00
Dining Out (Breakfast, Lunch, Dinner)	$250.00
Entertainment	$200.00
TOTAL	$4,960.00

→ *Tamecka's Total Monthly Spending*

YOUR MONEY-OUT LIST (AMOUNTS)

TOTAL MONTHLY SPENDING (MONEY OUT)

MONEY OUT (NAME)	MONEY OUT (AMOUNT)
	$
	$
	$
	$
	$
	$
	$
	$
	$
	$
	$
	$
	$
	$
	$
	$
	$
	$
	$
	$
	$
	$
	$
TOTAL	$

Budget Building Step 4: Calculate Your Beginning Savings

You may have heard me talk about this next step as "tears and tissues time" because what you're about to discover might come as a disappointment. But brace yourself and do the simple math to calculate how much of that Total Monthly Take-Home pay is left once you subtract your Total Monthly Expenses and spending. The number you get is what I call your Beginning Monthly Savings.

This calculation can reveal an uncomfortably clear financial picture—perhaps that you don't have much money available for savings at all. Even if you know money is tight, there's always a little room for some denial. But math doesn't do denial. It objectively displays the truth, even when the truth is inconvenient and uncomfortable.

And getting acquainted with this number presents an incredible opportunity for growth because it represents a significant milestone: You have created a basic budget. And that's big! You've poured a financial foundation on which you can build. You should be proud of yourself for doing the work to get here.

DO THE WORK ························➤

Think you're alone in cringing at discovering in hard numbers what you are saving every month? Think again! Take a look at Tamecka's example below and you'll see that she has more spending than money once she's done her math. Now calculate your Beginning Monthly Savings.

TAMECKA'S MONEY LIST – BEGINNING SAVINGS	
TOTAL MONTHLY TAKE-HOME PAY (MONEY IN)	$4,150.00
TOTAL MONTHLY SPENDING (MONEY OUT)	$4,960.00
	subtract
BEGINNING SAVINGS AMOUNT	-$810.00

Tamecka's Beginning Savings

YOUR MONEY LIST – BEGINNING SAVINGS	
TOTAL MONTHLY TAKE-HOME PAY (MONEY IN)	$
TOTAL MONTHLY SPENDING (MONEY OUT)	$
	subtract
BEGINNING SAVINGS AMOUNT	$

Budget Building Step 5: Assign Control Categories to Your Expenses

One of the most empowering and essential steps you can take toward bettering your financial life is to identify which expenses are in your control and which ones aren't. This sounds pretty basic, I know. But when people feel helplessness around money matters, it's often because they don't know the numbers they're dealing with or where they can make adjustments to create real change. The last step gave you the essential number to know—your Beginning Savings—and now we are going to identify where you can make changes if you want to improve that number.

You'll accomplish this by assigning what I call control categories to your expenses. These vary based on how much flexibility you have around paying an expense. Here are the three control categories:

- **Bills (B):** These are largely fixed expenses like rent, mortgage, credit card minimum payments, car payments, student loans, and insurance. If you didn't pay a bill with a capital B, you would likely have a collection agency coming after you. **Level of control: Low**
- **Utility Bills (UB):** Utility bills are what you pay for things like gas, electricity, and water, and they fluctuate since they're determined by your usage. You'd definitely have issues if you didn't pay these bills, but since your usage impacts your bill, I like to separate these from other bills. **Level of control: Medium**

- **Cash Expenses (C):** Pretty much everything that doesn't fall into a B or UB category is going to be a cash expense. This doesn't mean you've paid actual cash for something—this simply means that it's a nonobligatory expense. In other words, you have no contractual or other type of obligation to pay these expenses. You *chose* them. Cash expenses include everything from hair care and entertainment to groceries and dining out. **Level of control: High**

Once you have your expenses tagged, I want you to add up how much you are spending in each category. The totals of your B, UB, and C expenses bring a truth to light about why you don't have as much money as you'd like (and how you can fix this): You're going to see in black and white whether you have a *don't-make-enough* issue or a *spend-too-much* issue. In other words, you're going to discover if you're living too extravagantly (spending too much) or if you need to figure out how to make more to cover even your baseline expenses (don't make enough).

If you're spending on mostly Bs and UBs, your obligatory expenses are eating up your income and you likely don't make enough—you will ultimately want to work on bringing in more money. If your coins are being spent on mostly Cs, these more flexible types of expenses are draining your balance and you probably fall into the spend-too-much camp—you likely need to make modifications in how much money is going out.

DO THE WORK ·······················➤

Take a look at the way Tamecka categorized her expenses below.

TAMECKA'S MONEY LIST WITH CONTROL CATEGORIES

TOTAL MONTHLY TAKE-HOME PAY (MONEY IN)	$4,150.00			
TOTAL MONTHLY SPENDING (MONEY OUT)	$4,960.00			
	subtract			
BEGINNING SAVINGS AMOUNT	-$810.00			

MONEY IN (NAME)	MONEY IN (AMOUNT)	MONEY OUT (NAME)	MONEY OUT (AMOUNT)	CATEGORY: B/UB/C
Salary from job	$3,200.00	Mortgage	$2,600.00	B
Lyft	$650.00	Car Note	$300.00	B
Etsy Shop	$300.00	Car Insurance	$235.00	B
		Student Loan (Federal)	$250.00	B
		Cell Phone	$150.00	B
		Internet	$80.00	B
		Visa	$195.00	B
		Mastercard	$50.00	B
		Store Credit Card	$75.00	B
		Utilities (Water, Gas, Electric)	$300.00	UB
		Groceries	$100.00	C
		Toiletries	$100.00	C
		Grooming (Haircut, Eyebrows, Nails)	$75.00	C
		Dining Out (Breakfast, Lunch, Dinner)	$250.00	C
		Entertainment	$200.00	C
TOTAL	$4,150.00		$4,960.00	

Now get out your Money List and assign to each expense a B for Bills, UB for Utility Bills, or C for Cash Expense. Remember to do your B's and UB's first, because every expense left over will be labeled a C. Tally up your totals and use this information to help determine if you have a don't-make-enough issue or a spend-too-much issue. Don't worry—whichever it is, I will help you create a Boost-Your-Beginning-Savings plan that's right for you.

YOUR MONEY LIST WITH CONTROL CATEGORIES

TOTAL MONTHLY TAKE-HOME PAY (MONEY IN)				
TOTAL MONTHLY SPENDING (MONEY OUT)				
	subtract			
BEGINNING SAVINGS AMOUNT				

MONEY IN (NAME)	MONEY IN (AMOUNT)	MONEY OUT (NAME)	MONEY OUT (AMOUNT)	CATEGORY: B/UB/C
	$		$	
	$		$	
	$		$	
	$		$	
	$		$	
	$		$	
	$		$	
	$		$	
	$		$	
	$		$	
	$		$	
	$		$	
	$		$	
	$		$	
TOTAL	$		$	

IRL STORY: WENDY, NEW YORK, NY

I was a train wreck. I was spending more money than I made and living above my means. I didn't know where my money was going; I didn't have a budget, and I had no emergency funds. I relied on my mother to bail me out every time I got into trouble.

Then I made a Money List to see what I regularly have coming in and especially what I was spending. This was an eye-opener, and I was so ashamed of what it showed at first. But it was helpful to see things in stark numbers.

By far the best thing I ever did was automate my bills and my savings straight from my paycheck. It is true that if you don't see it, you don't think about it—and I know that my bills are being paid on time. I check my budget weekly, and I know where every penny of my income is going.

I have taken charge of my money; I have an emergency fund, have invested some money, and have multiple savings accounts including a vacation account. I am still enjoying life, but I have learned that I can say, "No, that's not in my budget" to everyone. A person must use their budget as a living document and revisit it frequently!

Budget Building Step 6: Reduce Your Expenses as Needed and Look for Ways to Increase Your Income, Then Recalculate!

By scrutinizing how much of your spending is within or outside of your control, you should have a pretty good idea of whether you have a spend-too-much issue or a don't-make-enough issue. Now we can get into customized strategies to change your story and increase your savings. Let me tell you: This is when things get exciting! I know you might be thinking, *Excitement and budgeting? Tiffany, those things don't mix!* But so many people have applied these strategies and reported back on the life-changing differences they've experienced. Let's get to the strategies that will help *you*. Roll up your sleeves!

If You Spend Too Much

Your job is pretty simple: You need to identify where you can reduce your expenses. Start with your Cs, over which you have the most control, and then move along to UBs, then Bs. Here are some examples in each category:

Cash (C) Cuts:

- Cancel unused or lightly used subscriptions, such as those for music, news, or streaming services.
- Bring lunch from home at least every other day.
- Delete heavily used food delivery apps or set a limit on how many times a week you can use them.
- Stop online shopping for a minimum of one week—stretch it to two or three to see a more significant impact.
- Create a meal plan to help cut down on impulse grocery shopping.

Utility Bill (UB) Cuts:

- You aren't helpless when it comes to utilities! You can often negotiate with service providers and ask how you may be able to get efficiency discounts—for example, are there filters, insulation, valves, or other tools you can use in your home that may help you save money?
- Unplug any "vampire" energy users. Items that are plugged in 100% of the time use electricity even when they're not turned on. Consider unplugging these items, such as your TV, or plugging them into a power strip that you turn off each night.

Bill (B) Cuts:

- Be proactive! Call your insurance company to ask if lower rates are available. There may be a promotional rate available that they hadn't thought to apply to your case (or that they explained in a mailer . . . which you tossed out!). It never, ever hurts to ask.

- If you own your home, consider refinancing your mortgage rate to lower your monthly bill. You'll know this could apply to you if the average national interest rates are lower than the rate you locked in when you set up your mortgage. But pay attention—make sure you aren't getting a lower rate (hooray!) that will balloon up again (to maybe even higher than what you're paying now—boo!) after a certain amount of time. If you are a renter and are locked into a yearlong agreement, start thinking about moving to a less expensive place when your lease runs out. Maybe there's a cheaper place you could live, even temporarily, to allow for greater savings.

- Consider surrendering your car. When you surrender your car, its current value is applied toward your balance owed on the loan. While you will be responsible for any remaining balance, paying this amount may ultimately cost less than defaulting on your car loan. The latter can come with longer-term credit consequences. I know it might seem like an extreme move to surrender your car, but if funds are really tight, it may be an option worth exploring.

- Apply for a student loan deferment to give yourself some breathing room. This can be accomplished simply by contacting the loaning bank or organization to see if you qualify for a pause on payments.

If You Don't Make Enough

When I say "you don't make enough," I mean that the money you bring in every month doesn't cover your nonnegotiable expenses. That is, even if you spent less on things you can control, you'd still need to make more. Your job now is to determine ways to increase your income. I know this feels like a grind. I know because I was in your shoes once when I was a preschool teacher. I had to get creative to increase what was coming in the door. But I made it happen—and so can you! Here are some steps to take to increase income (read more about these and other similar strategies in the chapter on increasing your income).

- Ask for a raise. This might sound uncomfortable, but when you support your ask with reasons why you deserve that raise, you'll feel more confident in the request. The best way to support the rationale for a raise is to create a "brag book." This is a place—a physical journal, a Google doc, or a draft email—where you document your accomplishments, actions you've taken that have helped your company make or save money, or other ways you've added value. When you're ready to ask for a raise, go in with your supporting evidence and present your case.
- Get a side hustle. A side hustle is a great way to bring in some extra money. The best way to add this hustle in without overworking/straining yourself is to generate the money by doing something that either you are already trained in/have a degree or certification in or is aligned with your primary source of income. In other words, use your known or practiced skills first before trying to learn or train in something new. If you're a teacher, maybe you can tutor students on the side. If you're a musician, maybe you can give music lessons. If you love to play soccer, could you coach a club team one evening a week? Lean on the gig economy (e.g., Lyft, Uber, Instacart), too, if you can. This type of work can be easier to "clock into" when it's convenient for you.

These efforts can make a real change in your monthly Money-In List, which will have a real effect on your bottom line. But I know they can take time. And if you are in the middle of a tough transition, like coming out of a divorce or significant illness, time feels like it's moving through molasses (unless we're talking about how quickly a bill comes due; that time seems to come as quickly as your alarm clock rings every morning). All you can do is have a plan and do your best while following it.

One other thing: If you are broke-broke and you literally cannot stretch your cash far enough to cover all your bills, here's how you decide which ones to pay: Ask yourself, "If I don't pay for this thing, am I going to be unhealthy or unsafe?" Your answers will help you prioritize utility, grocery, and medication costs, and possibly choose not to pay a credit card bill temporarily.

If you are in a position where you cannot pay a bill, be up front and communicative about this by calling the company to let them know where you stand. You're better off having an uncomfortable conversation than taking the express lane to collections. Explain your situation and ask if there are any revised payment plans you can utilize while you are experiencing financial distress.

Remember that you don't have to go through this all alone. Talk to your financial bestie about what's going on, and also consider connecting to the Dream Catcher community found in the tool kit—there you will find thousands of people ready to offer tips and help lift you up!

DO THE WORK ·······················➤

If you have a spend-too-much issue, you've identified where you can make cuts to your expenses. Now adjust the numbers to generate an expected new Money-Out total, then recalculate your Beginning Savings. Keep modifying as needed to maximize this savings figure.

If you have a don't-make-enough issue, you've worked to find ways to increase your income. If you have an anticipated pay increase or side-hustle earnings, add these to your Money-In column; recalculate your Beginning Savings.

Take a look at how Tamecka added income and reduced her spending on her Money List below, then use the blank sheet to make your own changes.

TAMECKA'S MONEY LIST (UPDATED INCOME & SAVINGS)

		WITH NEW INCOME & REDUCED SPENDING
TOTAL MONTHLY TAKE-HOME PAY (MONEY IN)	$4,150.00	$4,400.00
TOTAL MONTHLY SPENDING (MONEY OUT)	$4,960.00	$3,955.00
	subtract	subtract
BEGINNING SAVINGS AMOUNT	-$810.00	$445.00

MONEY IN (NAME)	MONEY IN (AMOUNT)	MONEY OUT (NAME)
Salary from Job	$3,200.00	Mortgage
Lyft	$650.00	Car Note
Etsy Shop	$300.00	Car Insurance
New Social Media Income	$250.00	Student Loan (Federal)
		Cell Phone
		Internet
		Visa
		Mastercard
		Store Credit Card
		Utilities (Water, Gas, Electric)
		Groceries
		Toiletries
		Grooming (Haircut, Eyebrows, Nails)
		Dining Out (Breakfast, Lunch, Dinner)
		Entertainment
TOTAL	$4,400.00	

MONEY OUT (AMOUNT)	CATEGORY: B/UB/C	MONEY OUT (REDUCED)
$2,600.00	B	$2,200.00
$300.00	B	$300.00
$235.00	B	$200.00
$250.00	B	$150.00
$150.00	B	$100.00
$80.00	B	$80.00
$195.00	B	$100.00
$50.00	B	$25.00
$75.00	B	$75.00
$300.00	UB	$300.00
$100.00	C	$100.00
$100.00	C	$100.00
$75.00	C	$50.00
$250.00	C	$75.00
$200.00	C	$100.00
$4,960.00		$3,955.00

YOUR MONEY LIST (UPDATED INCOME & SAVINGS)

		WITH NEW INCOME & REDUCED SPENDING
TOTAL MONTHLY TAKE-HOME PAY (MONEY IN)	$	$
TOTAL MONTHLY SPENDING (MONEY OUT)	$	$
	subtract	subtract
BEGINNING SAVINGS AMOUNT	$	$

MONEY IN (NAME)	MONEY IN (AMOUNT)	MONEY OUT (NAME)
	$	
	$	
	$	
	$	
	$	
	$	
	$	
	$	
	$	
TOTAL	$	

MONEY OUT (AMOUNT)	CATEGORY: B/UB/C	MONEY OUT (REDUCED)
$		$
$		$
$		$
$		$
$		$
$		$
$		$
$		$
$		$
$		$
$		$
$		$
$		$
$		$
$		$
$		$
$		$
$		$

Budget Building Step 7: Separate Your Funds

One way to get a better handle on your money is to make sure you can clearly see what it's doing. To help create clarity, I love a simple separation of funds into four different bank accounts. (If you followed the Quick Start at the beginning of the chapter, this will sound familiar.) Each account will serve a specific purpose. It's smart to have these accounts at different types of banks as they can offer you distinct benefits. See the online tool kit at madewholeworkbook.com for an updated list of my favorite banking institutions.

While it will take a little work to set up the accounts and get them running smoothly, I think you'll find it satisfying to boss your money around—"Yep, $30, you go here. And now you, $55, you go there." I'm not saying it's going to listen and grow into a million dollars overnight like you tell it to, but at least it can't talk back.

Here are the accounts I recommend you set up, along with where it's best to establish them.

Checking Accounts

Checking Account #1: Deposit/Spending Account

To be used for incoming money; for example, direct deposit take-home pay. You will want your debit card to be linked to this account as any C expenses will be paid out of it.

Get It Set Up: At a regular brick-and-mortar bank since this offers convenience and the option of an in-person visit if need be. If you already have it set up at an online bank or credit union, you can keep your account in place.

Checking Account #2: Bills Account

To be used only for money you will use to automatically or manually pay bills (aka, your B and UB expenses). This account should not be connected to a debit card—no need to accidentally swipe away your bill money! You will fund this account directly from your paycheck with the help of HR or with automatic or manual transfers from your checking account #1—more soon on how to ensure that you get this part right.

Get It Set Up: At the same brick-and-mortar bank as your checking account #1 for immediate and easy transfers.

Savings Accounts

Savings Account #1: Emergency/Short-Term Savings

This account will be used to build your emergency savings, which ideally will hold enough funds to cover three to twelve months' worth of your essential expenses. Your essential expenses will include things like utilities, rent or mortgage payments, groceries, and insurance. In the next chapter, I will help you zero in on your precise emergency savings needs.

Get It Set Up: Online-only savings accounts (offered by online-only banks) typically offer the highest interest rate and lowest required amount to open the account. Online-only banks can offer more competitive rates and lower costs to customers as they don't have the overhead that brick-and-mortar banks do.

Savings Account #2: Goal/Long-Term Savings (Money Bucket)

This account should be used to collect money to meet long-term goals. I'm thinking things like a trip, a down payment on a house, or your wedding and honeymoon (whether it's a year away or just a dream for someday). Think of this account as a bucket you might put out to collect rain in. If you don't put out the bucket, the rain is absorbed into the ground and it's gone—same with your cash. If you have some money coming in, it's going to get absorbed right into your everyday expenses if you don't have a plan for it, or rather, have a money bucket out to catch and save it! Want to go one step further? Set up several long-term savings accounts—that way, you have a "bucket" for each goal.

Get It Set Up: An online-only savings account is best here as well.

DO THE WORK ···················➤

Continue to use your Money List to keep track of which expenses will be paid from which account. Not sure how to do it? No worries! Use our girl Tamecka's completed Money List to help. I've even added a due date column to help you make sure you know when expenses need to be paid.

TAMECKA'S MONEY LIST WITH BANK ACCOUNTS

		WITH NEW INCOME & REDUCED SPENDING
TOTAL MONTHLY TAKE-HOME PAY (MONEY IN)	$4,150.00	$4,400.00
TOTAL MONTHLY SPENDING (MONEY OUT)	$4,960.00	$4,400.00
	subtract	subtract
BEGINNING SAVINGS AMOUNT	-$810.00	$0.00 ($0, because excess is now going to savings)

MONEY IN (NAME)	MONEY IN (AMOUNT)	MONEY OUT (NAME)
Salary from Job	$3,200.00	Mortgage
Lyft	$650.00	Car Note
Etsy Shop	$300.00	Car Insurance
New Social Media Income	$250.00	Student Loan (Federal)
		Cell Phone
		Internet
		Visa
		Mastercard
		Store Credit Card
		Utilities (Water, Gas, Electric)
		Groceries
		Toiletries
		Grooming (Haircut, Eyebrows, Nails)
		Dining Out (Breakfast, Lunch, Dinner)
		Entertainment
		NEW SAVINGS
TOTAL	$4,400.00	

MONEY OUT (AMOUNT)	CATEGORY: B/UB/C	MONEY OUT (REDUCED)	NAME OF ACCOUNT	DUE DATE
$2,600.00	B	$2,200.00	Bills	1st
$300.00	B	$300.00	Bills	28th
$235.00	B	$200.00	Bills	15th
$250.00	B	$150.00	Bills	5th
$150.00	B	$100.00	Bills	26th
$80.00	B	$80.00	Bills	28th
$195.00	B	$100.00	Bills	16th
$50.00	B	$25.00	Bills	16th
$75.00	B	$75.00	Bills	8th
$300.00	UB	$300.00	Bills	5th
$100.00	C	$100.00	Deposit/Spending	N/A
$100.00	C	$100.00	Deposit/Spending	N/A
$75.00	C	$50.00	Deposit/Spending	N/A
$250.00	C	$75.00	Deposit/Spending	N/A
$200.00	C	$100.00	Deposit/Spending	N/A
	C	$445.00	Emergency Saving	N/A
$4,960.00		$4,400.00		

YOUR COMPLETED MONEY LIST WITH BANK ACCOUNTS

		WITH NEW INCOME & REDUCED SPENDING
TOTAL MONTHLY TAKE-HOME PAY (MONEY IN)	$	$
TOTAL MONTHLY SPENDING (MONEY OUT)	$	$
	subtract	subtract
BEGINNING SAVINGS AMOUNT		**$0.00 ($0, because excess is now going to savings)**

MONEY IN (NAME)	MONEY IN (AMOUNT)	MONEY OUT (NAME)
	$	
	$	
	$	
	$	
	$	
	$	
	$	
	$	
	$	
TOTAL	$	

MONEY OUT (AMOUNT)	CATEGORY: B/UB/C	MONEY OUT (REDUCED)	NAME OF ACCOUNT	DUE DATE
$		$		
$		$		
$		$		
$		$		
$		$		
$		$		
$		$		
$		$		
$		$		
$		$		

DAYDREAM BREAK

Write down one budget-friendly way you'll celebrate after your budget is running smoothly. Make it worth it!

_____

_____

_____

Budget Building Step 8: Get Automated

Now that you've set up all your accounts, your final budgeting action is automation. Hallelujah for automation! It is hands down one of the best innovations in the digital age. And getting automated has never been easier.

To set up automation, you'll first go to your employer and ask that your direct deposit be split into multiple accounts. Revisit your newly created budget to confirm the amounts you want to go to your two checking accounts—one for cash expenses and the other for bills—and your two (or more) savings accounts for short-term and long-term savings. If you are self-employed or your employer cannot split your paycheck into multiple accounts, look into whether your bank has an auto-transfer system, or set a reminder for yourself (on your email or phone) to manually transfer money yourself.

The next step is to enroll in autopay for your recurring bills. Doing this with your mortgage/rent, car payments, cell phone bill, and so on will ensure that you never pay late fees or miss a payment. Of course, be sure to schedule the autopay payments to go out *after* your paycheck is deposited! If your income is more irregular, you may want to avoid setting up autopay—but you can take advantage of creating online accounts so that you can make payments quickly and from anywhere (as long as you have a smartphone).

DO THE WORK ·····················➤

Use this checklist to help you identify automation categories and track your progress.

AUTOMATION CHECKLIST

Automation Categories	✓	Notes
Income		
Will do one day		
Done		
Not relevant for me		
Direct deposit		
Will do one day		
Done		
Not relevant for me		
Bills (if you're certain you'll have your income every month)		
Will do one day		
Done		
Not relevant for me		
Savings—split it before you get it		
Will do one day		
Done		
Not relevant for me		

(table continues)

AUTOMATION CHECKLIST

Automation Categories	✓	Notes
Investments—automate retirement savings into an employer-sponsored account or your own investing account (more on investing in Chapter 7)		
Will do one day		
Done		
Not relevant for me		
Donating/tithing/philanthropy		
Will do one day		
Done		
Not relevant for me		

The Budget Building Review

In this chapter, you learned how to take a close look at your income, expenses, and savings to create a budget, the foundation on which you will build the rest of your financial life. If you have completed these steps, your baby budget has grown up! It's no small feat to make your money matters mature.

10% FINANCIALLY WHOLE

Guess what? You are now 10% financially whole. Big congratulations are in order!

10%
WHOLE

CHAPTER 3

20% Whole
Save Like a Squirrel

If you've ever saved money in order to do or acquire something—like go on a trip or buy a TV or those fancy shoes you've wanted for so long—you know what it's like to establish a savings goal and create and follow a plan to achieve that goal. This shows that you can keep your eyes on a prize in order to treat yourself.

But saving for and buying nonessential things is kind of like following a diet only to prep for a big event: a time-limited, goal-focused effort that you then ease up on when you've met your goal. I mean, you may have looked great in those wedding or high school reunion photos, but when you go back to eating junk food and sitting on the couch, you get unhealthy again.

Same with stashing away cash to pay for a onetime purchase—once you buy the *thing,* you don't keep saving. What you've done there is save to *spend money.* When you get good at saving, you'll create an intentional and consistent habit of saving money for specific goals as well as to support you in times of need. Ideally, you'll even start saving to *make money.*

To get good at saving this way, look no further than the humble backyard squirrel.

Squirrels never fail to hustle and stash food to carry them through the darkest and coldest winter months. They are super-savvy savers!

Squirrels are such smart savers because that's what they've been taught to do since they were little; their squirrel moms and dads made sure they knew how to save because it was a matter of survival. Many of us never had that kind of tutorial (about saving or budgeting or investing), and I'm trying to fix that!

The Plan to Save Like a Squirrel

The number one squirrel behavior we can model is to accept the certainty that winter is always coming—and then do the work during the abundant spring, summer, and fall months to prepare for it. A financial winter can show up in the form of a job loss or a significant health-, home-, or vehicle-related expense. If this "season" arrives suddenly and you aren't prepared, you'll have to scramble for money, and that can be stressful to say the least.

In this chapter, I'm going to coach you through the four steps of savings. You're going to learn to:

1. Identify and calculate your savings goal.
2. Drop down and get your noodle on (you'll soon learn what I mean by this!).
3. Practice mindful spending.
4. Set up and automate.

WHAT YOU'LL NEED

✓ An open mind, ready to explore and evolve your spending habits to prioritize saving
✓ The Money List you created on page 40
✓ A recent bank account and credit card statement

✓ Access to your online savings account—or if you don't already have one, a computer nearby that you can use to set up your account

Save Like a Squirrel Step 1: Identify and Calculate Your Savings Goal

In chapter 2, where we worked through the components of creating a budget, I introduced the idea that you should have two savings accounts, one for your emergency savings and another for your goal savings. Now it's time to identify how much you want to have in each account and the monthly amounts you need to save in order to get there.

Emergency Savings

An emergency savings account is the safety net of savings; it's what'll get you through the financial winter we just talked about. As in, if life knocks you down, it's there, at least financially speaking, to catch you. Scenarios where you might need to rely on your emergency savings include job loss, major unexpected vehicle or home issues, and sudden illness or injury. You can wish and pray with all your might that these things won't ever happen to you, but preparing for their *possibility* is the better strategy; being prepared is a precious gift you can give your future self.

What you need in your emergency savings: Money to cover at least three months' worth of your essential expenses (I call this meet-your-essential-needs budget your Noodle Budget; I'll teach you how to "get your noodle on" in the next step).

How to build up your emergency savings:

1. Do the simple math to determine your fixed expenses for three months.
2. Establish a realistic timeline for saving this amount to support you should you need it.

3. Identify the monthly contribution amount necessary to reach your goal within the set timeline.

4. Automate the monthly savings amount (see page 48).

DO THE WORK ·······················➤

For your emergency savings: Take a look at the Money List you created on page 40 and total up one month's worth of B and UB expenses. Now multiply that number by three. This is your initial emergency savings goal. Ideally, you will want that stash to grow to cover however many months you think it would take you to regain your income if you lost your job. For example, nurses are almost always in high demand, so three months will likely be enough. If you have a job that's hard to replace, like Chief Smile Officer (an actual job title!), you'll want to aim for more like three to twelve months' worth of expenses.

My initial emergency savings goal is: _____

Goal Savings

Emergency needs savings is only one piece of the savings picture. Another piece of it is setting aside money (aka saving!) to help fund your investing strategies, and we'll get to this in chapter 7. Saving first for these purposes is the responsible, adult thing to do. But guess what? We adults want to have fun and fund our more immediate dreams, too, right? That's why I'm also going to help you carve out a way to save for a desired purchase, whatever that may be. Got your eye on a Caribbean trip next spring? Is your all-time-favorite recording artist coming to town next summer? Do you want to put a down payment on a house? These are all legit desires, so let's figure out how to pay for them.

How to build up your goal savings:

1. Identify what you want to save for and do some research to get an estimated total cost.
2. Determine the date by which you want to have your money saved.
3. Calculate the monthly amount you need to put away to meet your goal.
4. Automate a monthly savings amount (see page 48).

DO THE WORK ·······················➤

Consider what you want to save for. Again, this might be a trip you want to take, a new piece of furniture or exercise equipment, a down payment on a home, or even a pair of shoes you want to buy. Establishing and building goal savings can help curtail impulse buys and avoid creating or adding to costly credit card debt (i.e., the kind you have to carry and pay interest on).

My initial goal savings goal is: _____

I'm saving for: _____

Save Like a Squirrel Step 2: Drop Down and Get Your Noodle On

Now that you know how much money you need to save monthly to meet your savings goals, you might be wondering where that money is going to come from. For some, it may be a simple matter of redirecting funds from your Beginning Savings total into your new savings accounts. For others, well, you might have to get a little extra squirrelly and work to gather those acorns. No matter which group you fall into, it's essential to get to know what I call your Noodle Budget, because even if you don't need it now, there may be a time when you do.

A Noodle Budget is the minimum amount of money you would need to keep you and your family healthy and safe. It's your lean-and-mean, meet-your-essential-needs-only budget. I call it the Noodle Budget because there are few things less expensive than the old-school twenty-four-pack of ramen noodles. So, if you were to think about surviving on just ramen, what would your financial bottom line look like?

> **TIFFANY TIP:** Of course, you don't have to actually like or live off ramen to get to know your Noodle Budget. In fact, if it helps, you can rebrand the budget to meet your inexpensive meal of choice—maybe yours is a Rice and Beans, PB&J, or Generic Cereal and Milk Budget. Whatever you call it, it's what's for dinner . . . and breakfast . . . and lunch in this imagined minimum spending scenario.

The hope is that you never have to live on your Noodle Budget. But knowing how much you would need to make it through a challenging time gives you a plan to fall back on (*Pssst—plans come with peace of mind!*) and a sense of where you can tighten your budget, even temporarily, to increase your monthly savings contributions. It helps to know that if and when the time comes, you can drop down and get your noodle on.

DO THE WORK ·······················➤

Take a look at the Money-Out List you created on page 24. Now prepare yourself to perform a soul-searching, line-by-line review of your spending. For each item, ask yourself three questions:

1. Do I need this expense to maintain my health and safety?
2. Am I contractually obligated to pay this expense?
3. If I don't pay it, will my credit score be impacted?

If the answer to any of these questions is no, this expense is *not* essential and should not make it into your Noodle Budget. If the answer to any of these questions is yes, put the expense to two further tests. Ask yourself:

1. Can I temporarily live without this expense and still maintain my health and safety?
2. Can I temporarily live without this expense without breaching the contract I've made with the company or lender?

If the answer to these second-tier questions is no, this is an essential expense and should be a line item on your Noodle Budget. If the answer to these questions is yes, it's not an absolutely essential—Noodle Budget–level—expense.

Now you've got your bare-bones, what-I'd-need-if-I-had-no-income-for-a-while budget. Do me a favor—take a look at the difference between this number and the number in your regular, this-is-what-I-usually-spend budget. Big difference? If so, you now know that as long as you've got your income, there are probably a number of ways you can start to spend less and save more, right? Just sayin'. Something to think about!

> **TIFFANY TIP:** I practice and preach the habit of identifying and using what I call Unexpected Money, aka UM. UM is any money that comes to you, well, unexpectedly. This could be a surprise rebate or refund, getting treated to a meal or outing that you were planning on paying for, finding a forgotten stash of cash, or receiving a discount on an item for which you thought you would need to pay full price. As soon as you get this money (or identify it, in the case of not having to pay full price for something), you should think of it as belonging to your financial future—if your emergency savings still needs funding, deposit it straight there. If not, transfer it into your goal savings or accelerate the paydown of a balance owed by adding it to a debt you're focused on paying down (we'll get to debt in the next chapter). Make Unexpected Money work for you! It can really add up.

Save Like a Squirrel Step 3: Practice Mindful Spending

Another way to help create a greater awareness of where there could be room for more saving in your life is to practice mindful spending. This isn't hard—you just need to ask yourself some simple questions before you buy something:

Do I need it?
Do I love it?
Do I like it?
Do I want it?

Asking these questions in this order will help you pause before buying something. Even a small pause for this reflection can prevent mindless or automatic spending. These questions were so helpful to me that I had them printed on stickers for my Dream Catcher community. We call them "deactivation stickers" because when you put them on your credit cards, you pause before you pay! The green bracelets on my arm on the book cover have the questions on them as well. These visual reminders helped my community stay on track, and I hope just asking the question of yourself will help you too.

Let's look at how you can define needs, loves, likes, and wants.

Needs provide shelter, food, or basic clothing. (The difference between basic and extra clothing is that basic threads are the ones that you wear all the time and that are likely to provide value for many years to come.)

Loves provide long-term enjoyment; you will feel the positive effects of these purchases years from now.

Likes provide short-term enjoyment, a little like the spending version of a sugar rush—it feels good at first, but that feeling doesn't last past a few months.

Wants provide little legitimate or lasting joy; they are often space-filling items that you buy automatically or impulsively.

Learning to distinguish among these categories and spending more on your needs and loves and less on your likes and wants will create opportunities for you to live more of the life you really desire.

DO THE WORK ·····················➤

Think about the four categories of needs, loves, likes, and wants and what falls into each category for you and write down some that come to mind. Though most people who do this exercise have the same things listed as "needs," from there people's definitions of loves, likes, and wants always varies. Commit to spending a little time figuring out what falls into each group for you. Skip Netflix for a night and just get to know your spending self a little better! It will be worth it.

My Needs:

_____

_____

_____

_____

_____

_____

My Loves:

_____

_____

_____

_____

_____

_____

_____

My Likes:

_____

_____

_____

_____

_____

_____

My Wants:

_____

_____

_____

_____

_____

_____

IRL STORY: CHANDRA, NEW YORK, NY

I always had some sort of savings, but it was not my priority. I had no budget to speak of, so I had no idea what I could intentionally save. For instance, I had no concept of creating a travel fund.

The first thing I did was set up a high-yield savings account. I moved my little savings out of my brick-and-mortar bank account and set up automatic withdrawals of about $100 per month from my checking account #1 into this high-yield savings account. I felt that was all I could handle at the time.

Then, any additional money that I came across via bonuses and/or my "Big Fat Check" via Rakuten would be deposited into the same account. Anytime I sold something online, I put that money into the high-yield savings account too. I did not care if it was $2 or $20. I sold clothes, books, old textbooks, CDs (yes, I said CDs). If I did any type of gig work, that money went to savings too.

My life has totally changed. As I made more money, I got into the habit of saving 10% of my income (at minimum) and all Unexpected Money. I now have more money saved than I have had most of my adult life, and instead of spending it on shiny new things, I invest on a monthly basis. I learned that you have to tell your money where to go or it will go wherever it wants to.

Also, I still have the original Need it? Love it? Like it? Want it? sticker from The Budgetnista on one of my credit cards!

Save Like a Squirrel Step 4: Set Up and Automate

I hope you've already set up two savings accounts, but if not, let's recap exactly what you need and where to get this done.

When you borrow money from a bank (like for a mortgage or other loan), they ask you to pay interest on the amount you borrow over the course of the loan. When you stash money at a bank, you are effectively *loaning it to the bank* (since they have access to it while they are holding it for you) and so *they* should pay *you* interest on that loan! When opening your savings accounts, you want to look for the highest interest rate possible (which is obviously very different from when you borrow—that's when you want a low rate). This bank should offer a high-yield savings account (HYSA), have a grade A, be insured by the FDIC (Federal Deposit Insurance Corporation), have a low minimum opening deposit, and have no balance requirement. I keep an updated list of my top picks in the *Made Whole* tool kit online at madewholeworkbook.com.

Maybe you're rolling your eyes and thinking, *But, Tiffany, I already* have *a savings account with my bank—why are you making me do extra work?* I'll tell you why: Money in a savings account that's attached to your checking account is more available to you—and that's a bad thing. We want your savings to be inconvenient to access. Because inconvenient money is safe from reckless and routine spending. It doesn't get transferred to your checking account with one simple click and swallowed up in the black hole of impulse buys.

But don't worry—transferring money/having money automatically transferred to your online savings account doesn't mean it's *totally* inaccessible. It's still there if you absolutely need it. Online banks offer quick-ish transfers so that you can access your money within twenty-four to seventy-two hours.

DO THE WORK ·······················➤

Once you've created your savings accounts at a separate bank, one for emergencies and one for goals, you will want to link these to your checking account #1. I know I said I don't want to make transfers between checking and savings easy, but we do need to make it possible. So allowing your two banks to talk to each other will allow you to start transferring funds from your checking account into both savings accounts. These transfers will typically take a day or two versus the milliseconds they would if your money were all at the same bank. It's important that it's not quick and easy to transfer your money from savings to checking, for spending. FYI, if you know that you will have reliable income, it's time to set up automated transfers from checking to savings.

The Save Like a Squirrel Review

Getting good at saving starts with learning from super-savvy saving squirrels; they stash acorns to help them endure winter, and we should do the same with our cash to make sure we can make it through any financial downturn.

Getting good at saving also means identifying your Noodle Budget and establishing an emergency savings and a goal savings and automating transfers into these accounts to help them grow. When you set up these savings habits and keep them in place, you will give yourself the priceless gifts of preparedness and peace of mind!

20% FINANCIALLY WHOLE

Congratulations! You have accomplished 20% financial wholeness.

CHAPTER 4

30% Whole
Dig Out of Debt

We've covered budgets and savings, and I hope you're feeling a little more in control of your finances. Because you're already 20% whole!

But now we come to everyone's least favorite topic: debt. If you've got debt—and most of us have some—you're likely not super proud of it. You've probably kept the total amount of debt that you have a secret from others. Maybe you've even avoided adding up how much debt you have as a way to sort of keep it a secret from yourself too!

But you know what? When you focus on solutions, you don't have time for secrets. What you need is a plan for paying down your debt. I promise you'll feel a whole lot better once you do. And here's something you might be relieved to hear me say: You don't have to be 100% debt free before you can be financially whole. Paying off your debt is *a* goal, but it's not *the* goal. Once you have a plan in place and begin to chip away at what you owe to creditors, you'll feel a weight starting to lift. It's gonna be good!

> **TIFFANY TIP:** If you talk about debt as though it's something you're *in*, it's time to change your vocab. Here's why: Debt is not a place. Yet when you make it one, it becomes somewhere you can get stuck. A more positive way to talk about debt is to simply say, "I have a debt to pay." That's accurate, and it leaves room for action!

The Plan to Dig Out of Debt

This chapter will guide you through the four steps to digging out of debt:

1. Identify your debt.
2. Restructure your debt.
3. Choose a paydown plan.
4. Automate the paydown plan.

WHAT YOU'LL NEED

✓ The most recent statements from all the accounts on which you owe, such as credit cards, your car loan, school loans, and your mortgage

✓ Any personal notes that reflect money you've borrowed and the balances you owe

✓ Kindness and patience. Making yourself feel bad about your debt is not going to be helpful. Instead, I want you to celebrate the awareness and focus on doing the work.

Dig Out of Debt Step 1: Identify Your Debt

Listen, it's impossible to create a plan to address something without really knowing what you're dealing with. That's why we're going to start with identifying your debt. You're going to look it straight in the eye by creating a simple and straightforward Debt List to help you catalog all the important details.

I want to point out to the debt-dreaders out there that this is a list of *information*, not of emotion, and definitely not of judgment. I know—believe me, I *know*—from personal experience how heavy debt dread can feel. But the road to feeling better about it starts with collecting the stats you need so you can create a plan. If you're an Excel person, this list is going to have seven cells. If you compile data old-school, that simply means the list has seven components. Those are:

1. Name of Debt

You can't fix it if you can't name it! Start with the name of the person or entity that you owe or a description of what's owed.

2. Total Amount Owed

However much you may avoid looking at this number, this is also a straightforward piece of data: the current total amount you owe to the person or entity listed above (*not* the beginning balance or original amount borrowed).

3. Minimum Monthly Payment

All commercial bills or invoices will itemize the minimum amount you need to pay to avoid a late fee. Creditors do this based on the contract you've entered with them, but sometimes this also makes people like you and me see that lower number—the minimum due—and think that's all we have to pay. We might not realize that we will continue to have to pay interest on the remaining "total amount due" and that if we only ever pay the minimum to avoid the late fee, we aren't making much progress on the total amount due. But they aren't fooling you anymore!

For most debts, the minimum payment will be a monthly payment. However, if you're making payments on money borrowed from a friend or family member, your terms might be different. In that case, just divide the total amount due by twelve to calculate what your payment would break down to monthly.

4. Total Interest

As you're probably aware (though not everyone is!), creditors charge you interest on the amount you owe them. That's called the "interest rate." Some creditors also charge you an "annual percentage rate" (APR). If this extra fee is part of the deal, they will list an APR instead of an interest rate. The interest rate is the cost you will pay each year to borrow the money, expressed as a percentage rate. The APR is basically a figure that reflects how much it costs you to borrow money from a company.

The interest rate and APR will be clearly listed on your statement. For the sake of your Debt List, if your debt comes with an APR, add that to the Interest column on your Debt List. If not, write in the interest rate provided.

5. Due Date

This is the date your payment is due. Straightforward, right? Maybe not! Keep in mind that due dates are time-zone specific. So if you're in California on Pacific Standard Time and your credit card or mortgage company is on the East Coast, your 9:01 p.m. payment might miss the midnight Eastern Standard Time cutoff for on-time payments. Check your statement to make sure you document the due date *and* time. Don't pay a late fee unnecessarily!

6. Statement Date

The statement date is when your monthly interest charge and minimum payments are calculated, and when your bill is typically generated. This is an important date to be aware of not only so you know when to expect the next bill but also because this is the date when your balance is sent to the credit bureaus. (More on credit in the next chapter.)

7. Status

Are you current or behind on your payments? Make note of that here. This is also the place to add if you have a promotional rate (e.g., a low interest rate that lasts only for a specified amount of time before it goes up—sometimes waaaay up!) and when that rate expires.

DO THE WORK ·······················➤

Here's what a completed Debt List looks like:

COMPLETED DEBT LIST

NAME OF DEBT	TOTAL AMOUNT OWED	MIN. MONTHLY PAYMENT	INTEREST
Mortgage	$320,000.00	$2,200.00	6.00%
Car Note	$22,000.00	$300.00	6.00%
Visa	$5,000.00	$60	18.99%
Store Credit Card	$650.00	$75	24.75%
Mastercard	$2,000.00	$25	15.00%
Student Loans (Federal)	$35,000.00	$150.00	5.5%

Complete your own here (access a downloadable version at madewholeworkbook.com):

COMPLETED DEBT LIST

NAME OF DEBT	TOTAL AMOUNT OWED	MIN. MONTHLY PAYMENT	INTEREST
	$	$	

DUE DATE	STATEMENT DATE	STATUS
1st	N/A	Current
28th	N/A	Current
16th	6th	1 month late
8th	1st	Current
22nd	12th	Delinquent
5th	N/A	Forbearance

DUE DATE	STATEMENT DATE	STATUS

DEBT COLLECTOR CONVERSATION CHECKLIST

If you have missed payments on your debt, you are either already getting calls from debt collectors or you soon will! These calls can be threatening and scary, but they'll just keep coming if you don't deal with them. If you know how to hold on to your power, you can take the call (rather than avoid it) and emerge from the conversation unscathed. Use this checklist to make sure you're ready.

- ☐ **I'm organized.** Have any relevant bills and notes (re: previous payments, dates, etc.) at your side before you get on the phone.

- ☐ **I'm calling them on my own terms.** Answer or return the call when you are calm and in a space where you have privacy.

- ☐ **I did my research, and I know my rights.** Review the Fair Debt Collections Practices Act (FDCPA) to make sure you're not being hounded by unfair debt collection practices. You can also send a cease and desist letter to make sure discussions take place on your terms, and request that your debt be validated in writing. See templates in the online tool kit.

- ☐ **I will not discuss payment or any details of the debt until I've received a debt validation letter.** In the beginning of every debt-collection process, a creditor will want you to agree to make a partial payment or issue a written or verbal promise to pay. If you accidentally do this with debt that's actually not yours or has expired, you can still be on the hook to pay. For this reason, you do not want to "own" the debt until there's proof that it belongs to you. Proof would come in the form of a debt validation letter; always ask for one before discussing details with a debt collector.

- ☐ **I will always ask for everything in writing.** You will never remember all the details, but they will, which is why you should request everything in writing.

- ☐ **I will remember that it's my job to look out for my own best interest.** A debt collector's job is to get you to admit to owing the debt and then commit to paying it. Your job is to make sure a debt collector is not using illegal tactics to coerce or harass you.

Dig Out of Debt Step 2: Restructure Your Debt

The goal of this step is to make paying down your debts easier and more economical. You can accomplish this by consolidating some debts and negotiating others. Let's look at what strategies work best with the three most common types of debt: credit card debt, student loan debt, and mortgage debt.

Credit Card Debt

If you are carrying credit card balances, I recommend you focus on these balances before any other debt. This is because credit card debt is expensive! Most credit card companies charge double-digit interest on the money you owe.

Restructuring Strategies

Negotiate a lower interest rate. Call your credit card company's customer service line and ask to speak to someone about getting a lower interest rate on what you owe. Yes, you really can do this! You won't always get a lower rate, but asking for it does no harm. Plus, if you let the customer service representative know that you are considering transferring your debt to another card company (see below), you have a little leverage. Why? Because a bank that is collecting money through your interest payments doesn't really want to lose you as a customer! You'd be surprised at how often they are willing to play ball with you.

Transfer your balance. Look around for lower or no-interest credit card promotions at other banks or companies. You might be able to get one and then transfer your current credit card balance to the new card. Essentially, this means you'll be paying off your current card with another one. But if the new card has a lower—or no—interest rate, you win because you'll have to pay less interest over time.

You obviously want to look for the lowest interest rate and lowest fees available, but make sure to pay attention to the amount of time that these promotional and low rates will last. Also pay attention to what the interest rate will be after the low-rate promotional period ends. Then do the math to figure out your best option. The best card of all will offer 0% interest on balance transfers along with no balance transfer fee, but unless you have an excellent credit rating, these offers can be hard to come by. Even with a transfer fee, a balance transfer may make sense for you. The only way to know for sure is to compare the cost of paying the interest charges on your current card with the cost of transferring the balance to a new card. Here's a sample calculation:

Your credit card balance: $8,000

The interest rate on your current card: 20%

Cost to keep the balance where it is: 8,000 × .20 = $1,600 in interest per year

Balance transfer offer: 0% interest for 12 months with a 3% fee

Cost to transfer the balance: 8,000 × .03 = $240

Comparison: $1,600 versus $240 and a year to pay it off

Analysis: It absolutely makes sense to transfer!

Note: It may not make sense to transfer if the amount you're allowed to transfer is significantly lower than what you owe.

Take out a personal loan. Remember that your goal is to make debt payment easier or more economical. If you can get a personal loan from a bank at a lower interest rate than your credit card, your debt has become less expensive to you—and that's a win. I recommend shopping for a personal loan like you would approach any other financial decision. You want to consider the interest rate and ideally look to borrow money from a bank that's been given a B+ or better grade by the FDIC, or Federal Deposit Insurance Corporation. You can visit FDIC.gov to review any company's grade.

If you think a personal loan might be right for you right now, a credit union is a great place to start your search. Because so many are nonprofit, they can offer lower repayment interest rates.

DO THE WORK ·····················➤

Keep notes on what you're up to by filling in the following info. Examples of an "Action" would be to negotiate, transfer, or pay with a personal loan.

Credit cards I'm looking to restructure:

Card: _____ Action(s): _____

Card: _____ Action(s): _____

Card: _____ Action(s): _____

Card: _____ Action(s): _____

Student Loan Debt

Student loans can weigh heavily on your shoulders. You're happy you got the education that came with them, but having to start paying them back right after you graduate can quickly cool those just-out-of-school jets! The best restructuring strategies for this type of debt really depend on a few facts: what type of loan you have—federal or private—and how many loans you have.

Restructuring Strategies for Federal Loans

Federal loans are funded by the government. If you have a federal loan, do not, I repeat, *do not* refinance. If you refinance, you give up protections that come with this type of loan.

For example, a federal student loan gives you access to a forbearance or a deferral, which are two types of delayed repayment options. These can save you big-time should you become unemployed or disabled or experience significant financial hardship. When you have a forbearance or deferral arrangement, you can miss nine payments before you are considered to have defaulted on the loan (a loan default is really bad for your credit score). If you refinance your federal loan, you lose this right.

If you work for a nonprofit or in another qualifying field, you also have the option of applying for loan forgiveness. And as we saw during the Covid-19 pandemic, the federal government paused federal student loan payments for years in an effort to help borrowers.

Restructuring Strategies for Private Loans

You can determine if you have a federal or private student loan by calling your lender to ask, but know that private loans are usually those that have been issued by a bank, credit union, school, or state agency (basically any entity other than the federal government).

If you have a private loan, you generally don't have any protections or forgiveness considerations. This means that if you miss one payment, you are in default. This type of loan is a good candidate for refinancing as you may be able to find a better rate.

DO THE WORK ·······················➤

Find out what kind of loan you have—private or federal—by calling your lender.

If You Have a Federal Loan

If you're struggling with repayment, ask about your delayed repayment options and/or any assistance programs that may be available.

If You Have a Private Loan

- Gather some key numbers:
1. Total student loan debt (private loans only) = _____
2. Average interest rate of these loans (add up your interest rates and divide by the number of private student loans you have) =

   _____
3. Credit score = _____

- Now check out my top picks for private student loan refinancing in the online tool kit at madewholeworkbook.com and start shopping for a better loan. Make note of your options here:

Bank name: _____

Interest rate: _____

Repayment period: _____

Mortgage Debt

If your goal is to lower your mortgage payment (I mean, who doesn't want to pay less in housing expenses?), you can explore the option of refinancing your loan. A refinance may make sense if you can lower your interest rate, but you will want to consider a few other factors, too, such as closing costs (insurance, taxes, escrow, title and lender fees) and the length of time you plan to own your home.

You can calculate whether or not refinancing makes sense by dividing the cost of closing by your monthly savings to see how long it would take for the new loan to pay for itself. Using an example where a new mortgage would save you $300 and the closing costs are $3,500:

$3,500 ÷ $300 monthly savings = 11.66 months

So, basically it would take you a year to break even. As a general rule of thumb, if the math doesn't pencil out to your recovering your closing costs in five years or less, pass on the refinance. If you plan to sell your home before you break even, it would not make sense to refinance.

There's another type of refinance called a cash-out refinance or home equity loan that some people find appealing, but it should be approached with caution. This option allows you to draw on the equity in your home (the difference between what you owe on your mortgage and what your home is currently worth). With this type of loan, you get a lump sum that you can spend on whatever you like (including paying off other debt), but it effectively becomes a second mortgage on your home. Since mortgage rates tend to be lower than rates on other types of debt, people will sometimes use this money as a way to pay off more expensive debt, like a credit card.

This sounds like a pretty great idea, right? But listen carefully: This should be the last line of your debt defense. Why? Because there are fees involved in a cash-out refinance that you may not have considered. Beyond and perhaps bigger than that, it can feel a little too easy to pay off high-interest credit card debt this way. Remember: When you relocate your credit card debt to mortgage debt, it's not resolved; you still have to repay somebody! But having transferred your debt to a lower interest lender sometimes *feels* like a resolution. This can lead to trouble because it opens the door to going right back out and racking up more credit card debt!

DO THE WORK ·····················➤

If you have a mortgage and you are considering a refinance, here's the calculation to use to see if it might make good financial sense for you:

Estimated closing costs (obtain these from the mortgage professional with whom you are working) =

Current mortgage _____ – New mortgage _____ = _____
                                                                monthly savings
                                                                potential

_____ closing costs/ _____ monthly savings = _____
                                                            number of months it
                                                            would take to break
                                                            even

IRL STORY: MALIK, HOUSTON, TX

At one point, I found myself $95,000 in credit card debt. I had no idea that I was actually in that much credit card debt because it was spread across several cards, and I was always able to keep up with my monthly payments.

My minimum monthly payment across all my cards was roughly $3,500 per month, and I was paying roughly $11,000 per year in interest across all these accounts (I learned this when tax time came). Plus, I still had car payments, rent, and other bills to pay, all while going through the emotional and financial woes of the pandemic.

Tiffany finally helped me get organized and create an actual plan to reduce and/or eliminate my credit card debt. She helped me:

1. Identify my debt. I was able to identify and understand whom I owed and how much I owed them. (I couldn't unsee it once I saw it!)
2. Restructure my debt. This step in the process forced me to look deeply into what options I had to lower the interest I was paying while still reducing and/or eliminating the debt itself.
3. Choose a paydown plan. Once I restructured my debt, I chose to pay it down.
4. Automate my paydown plan. Once the first three steps were done, I set monthly targets and automated the paydown. Once the automation was completed, I was able to focus on earning since all the other factors were addressed.

By following these steps, I was able to reduce my monthly overhead by $4,000! I also improved my credit score, moving it from in the 600s to over 800. I can now invest and save in a much more meaningful and intentional way, and I feel like a financial weight has been lifted and I am free.

Since paying down my debt, I have also been able to travel more and work less. Freeing myself from the credit card debt allowed me to reclaim more of my earnings and also my time, and it's given me the opportunity to focus on and do more of the things that make me happy.

Dig Out of Debt Step 3: Choose a Paydown Plan

If you pay your bills every month—on time and in the minimum needed amounts—good for you! That's a start. But that really also means that you're doing the *minimum* you can or should do to get rid of your debt. So now it's time to pick the best plan to use for *paying down* your debts. Shifting from just paying your bills to following a plan can help create momentum and give you some payoff wins that boost your motivation to keep going. And let's face it—no one is super eager to do the work it takes to pay down debt, so I say bring on any bit of motivation we can find!

The two most common paydown strategies used are called the Snowball Method and the Avalanche Method. Each method has unique benefits, and plenty of people have had success with both. Personally, I like a hybrid of the two. What's best for you will depend on a few factors, such as the amount of your debts and the corresponding interest rates, and your personality. Let's take a look at how these paydown methods work.

The Snowball Method

The Snowball Method has you pay off your debts from smallest to largest regardless of the interest rates for your various balances. The idea is that you create a "snowball" of paid-off debts that grows bigger and bigger as it rolls down a hill, building momentum.

The main benefit of this strategy is that by starting with your smallest debt, you can eliminate at least one debt relatively quickly and gain confidence in your ability to keep working your way down your debt list.

In practice, this method would have you:

1. Organize your debts from the smallest current balance to the largest.
2. Revisit your Money List to see how much money you can squeeze from your budget to repay debt.
3. Automate all your debt payments to minimum payment except for your smallest debt. To that one, you would add that extra amount of savings to the minimum payment until you have paid off the debt.
4. Roll the minimum payment and the extra money to the second smallest debt and begin paying that one down.

The Avalanche Method

With the Avalanche Method, your goal is to pay off your most expensive debt—that is, the debt with the highest interest rate (regardless of the total balance)—first. This means organizing your debts in order of highest to lowest interest rate and then following the same steps as you would with the Snowball Method: Pay the minimum payment for all your debts, but apply any additional money extracted from your budget to pay down the debt with the highest interest rate first. Once that is paid down, you jump to the next highest debt on your list.

The Avalanche Method gets debt paid down—no doubt about it—but that doesn't mean it's the best approach for everybody. The main downside to this approach is that it can take a long time to see a "win," and that can lead to feeling like you're never going to get out of debt—even if you're making very real incremental progress.

So consider your personality. Do you need quick wins to help you stay on track? Get started with the Snowball Method stat. Or can you go it slow and steady, gradually working your way toward what might be a bigger budgeting win? The Avalanche Method could be right for you.

As I mentioned earlier, I like a hybrid approach. This would have you pay off some of your smaller debts using the Snowball Method and then shift to the Avalanche

Method when it makes sense, such as when the interest rate on a debt is out of control. I like this combined approach because you get the immediate boost of confidence and feeling of accomplishment with the Snowball accounts but also see your higher-interest-rate debt getting smaller and smaller. This gives you a sense of accomplishment and builds your confidence, both of which can go a long way in helping diminish debt dread.

The best way to understand how to apply the combined approach is to take a look at a debt story to see how it works IRL. Let's see how Michelle used it to work down her debts.

Michelle's Debts

Credit card debt: $12,000
Minimum monthly payment due: $250
Interest rate: 22%

Personal loan: $2,500
Minimum monthly payment due: $50
Interest rate: 7%

Auto loan: $600
Minimum monthly payment due: $100
Interest rate: 6%

Pay Down Debt (PDD) number (extra monthly money found in budget to put toward debt paydown plan: $200

Michelle decided to start with the Snowball Method and focused on her auto loan first since it was the lowest debt. By adding $200 a month to her minimum monthly payment, she paid off this smaller loan in under two months. Hooray for quick wins!

With that done, she shifted the funds she had been applying to that debt (the $100 minimum payment and her $200 PDD number) to the next lowest debt, her personal loan. Once she paid that off, she decided it was time to switch to the Avalanche Method and focus on debt with the larger, high-interest balance, her credit card. Just like Michelle, you can do a mix and roll that Snowball right into an Avalanche.

Have you decided which debt repayment approach you're going to pick? Maybe a hybrid like Michelle's? If you are still unsure, you can check out a free Snowball or Avalanche calculator online (see the tool kit for some of my faves) to see how long it might take you to become debt free depending on the approach you're considering. Keep in mind that these calculators won't generate precise timelines if you're looking to use the hybrid approach.

One final note: Don't get stuck in the deliberating phase! Debts don't just get smaller on their own; they are resolved only through strategic and routine repayment. Pick an approach and get started knowing that you can modify it as you go.

DO THE WORK ·······················➤

Organize Your Debts

Use the Snowball Method to organize your debts from the smallest current balance to the largest:

DEBT LIST

NAME OF DEBT	TOTAL AMOUNT OWED	MIN. MONTHLY PAYMENT	INTEREST
	$	$	

DUE DATE	STATEMENT DATE	STATUS

Use the Avalanche Method to organize your debts from the highest interest rate to the lowest:

DEBT LIST

NAME OF DEBT	TOTAL AMOUNT OWED	MIN. MONTHLY PAYMENT	INTEREST
	$	$	

DUE DATE	STATEMENT DATE	STATUS

☐ I've organized my debts.

☐ I know my PDD number (the excess money from your budget after bills and obligations and savings each month).

☐ I've picked the debt I'm going to focus on first.

☐ I've established the date when I will start making my minimum payment plus my PDD number toward this debt.

☐ I've told my financial bestie about my plan; they're in the know and on my side!

Dig Out of Debt Step 4: Automate the Paydown Plan

You've done the hard work to create a plan, and now it's time to take one last easy step to ensure your success: automate! Automation is like a magical form of multitasking—in this example, your debts get paid down on autopilot while you get to focus on other areas of financial wholeness.

> **TIFFANY TIP:** If you've done the math to see how long it will take you to pay off your first debt, note this date in your calendar so you can make sure to roll those funds over to the next debt you need to tackle.

DO THE WORK ···············➤

Log in to the account of the debt you want to focus on first and set up automatic payments in the amount you can manage (your minimum payment plus PDD number). Once you've done that, grab your debt sheet and put an *A* next to the ones you've automated; this includes those on which you are paying just the minimum payment.

- ☐ I'm all set up on automatic payments. Go me!
- ☐ I've got all my debt payments automated!
- ☐ I've got a few stragglers that I still need to get set up, but here's the date by which I will have all my debts automated: _____
- ☐ I'm still struggling to get all my debts in a row and a payment plan in place.

If you checked this last box, I see you. I've been there, and I know how tough it can be to climb out if you're in the deep end of debt. This is when I really want you to lean on your financial bestie. Remember, money is a team sport—you are not supposed to do it alone (more on this in chapter 10). Call your bestie and get your grief out into the open; let that debt burden breathe a little by talking about it. And if you haven't found anyone you can lean on for support in this area, I've got thousands of Dream Catchers who regularly connect, commiserate, and congratulate one another on their financial lives—join them via the link shared in the tool kit.

The Dig Out of Debt Review

You've done the tough work of confronting and calculating your debt and creating a plan to pay it down. Completing these steps can set you on course to eliminate your most expensive debt, which can free up funds to put toward saving and investing. Remember that debt freedom isn't the ultimate goal; financial wholeness is.

30% FINANCIALLY WHOLE

You are now 30% financially whole. You are making moves, *big* ones, to better your life. I'm forever here cheering you on!

CHAPTER 5

40% Whole
Score High (Credit)

I know that for many people, trying to figure out credit feels just about as easy as trying to figure out calculus. I've heard all the questions:

What factors influence my credit score?

How can I increase my score?

What's up with the bureaus that issue credit scores?

Does my cholesterol affect my credit score?

(OK, maybe not this last one—but sometimes it feels like *everything* makes a difference in your score!)

The good news is, if you've got credit questions, I've got the answers. And we're going to get right to them in this chapter. Let's dive in (don't worry, we'll start at the shallow end!).

The Plan to Score High (Credit)

Your goal at this stage is to grow your FICO (Fair Isaac Corporation) score. I'll explain what the heck that means in a minute, but know that you're looking to get it to 740 or higher. To achieve this goal, you're going to go through five steps:

1. Check your payment history.
2. Reduce your amounts owed and improve your credit utilization.
3. Identify the length of your credit history/hack your age.
4. Protect your credit inquiries.
5. Manage your credit mix.

WHAT YOU'LL NEED

- ✓ An understanding of the basics of credit reporting. Read on below!
- ✓ Your credit report—your bank and credit card companies likely offer free credit reports, and you can also use AnnualCreditReport.com.
- ✓ Your credit score—not all credit reports will show your score, so make sure you have one that does. Specifically, find your FICO score. Look for the three-digit number ranging from 300 to 850.

Quick Start: Jump Like Jordan

I call this my "Jump Like Jordan" (as in iconic NBA player Michael Jordan) tip because it can make your score jump!

Because your credit score is affected by how consistently you pay off your debts, you are going to completely pay off one small credit card balance every month. Here's a more detailed look at how this is done:

1. Check out your monthly bills on your Money List. Find the smallest recurring bill, likely a streaming service of some kind.

2. Identify a credit card of yours that has a $0 balance, or get your credit card to a $0 balance.

3. Move the smallest recurring bill to this card and have it automatically charged there. This is your Jump Like Jordan credit card. This small monthly bill should be the *only* thing this card is used for, so leave it at home.

4. Set up your checking account #2 to pay off this card each month after the statement closing date. Make sure it's set to pay off your debt *after* the statement date, so you know that your low credit usage has been reported to the credit bureaus. And pay it *by* the due date so you're not late.

5. Then don't mess with your success! Let this charge and payoff system run automatically as you reap the benefits of the credit score boost.

Let's Begin with the Credit Basics

First things first, let's establish what we are talking about when we talk about credit. Credit is currency that you have access to with strings attached. The main string being that you have to pay the money back and meet the terms of repayment. For example, when you are approved for a credit card with a limit of, say, $3,000, a bank is basically saying to you, "We will give you $3,000 in credit, but we'll charge you interest until you pay us back."

Credit is also used as a descriptor of the way you pay what you owe. If you pay your bills on time, you can be described as having good credit. If you don't, you might be said to have bad credit. ("Good" and "bad" aren't used as a character judgment; they are strictly related to your ability to pay back loans.)

Your history of repayment and your overall management of credit will generate what's referred to as your credit score, and the higher the number, the better. But that number (score) isn't the only "player" you need to understand. There's also your credit report and the credit bureaus, and it's important to know a little bit about each. I like to think of these in terms we're all familiar with from high school: your grade point average (GPA), your transcript, and your teachers.

Your Credit Score = Your GPA

Your credit score is a three-digit, computer-generated number that is designed to calculate the chance that you will pay back a debt that's owed. And in the simplest terms, it's a number that tells lenders how close to or far away from bankruptcy you are. The lower your score, the more likely you are to file for bankruptcy and the less likely a lender is to get back the money that they lend you. A higher credit score means that you are considered a lower-risk borrower who is likely to repay debt. A good credit score can open doors in the areas of employment, homeownership, and more.

Your credit score is made up of five factors: payment history, credit utilization, credit inquiries, credit history, and credit mix. The great news is that this gives you a handful of areas where you can focus your efforts to improve your score; we'll go through each factor and how to prioritize your efforts a little later in this chapter!

There are a few different credit scoring models, but we're going to focus on the FICO score because it's the most recognized. A FICO score ranges from 300 to 850. According to MyFICO.com, these are the credit score ranges and the associated ratings. The rating is related to how a lender might perceive you as a borrower and the likelihood that they will lend to you.

FICO Score Ranges	Rating
300–580	Poor
580–669	Fair
670–739	Good
740–799	Very Good
800–850	Exceptional

Your Credit Report = Your Transcript

Similar to how a high school transcript shows the classes you took and how you performed (i.e., your grades), a credit report will show the credit for which you've been approved and how it was managed. Every credit account that's been created and connected to your name and Social Security number will appear on this report, along with the payment history and status of each account. And when I say every credit account, I mean every one—credit cards, mortgages, bankruptcies, liens, and collections all will appear on your credit report. Although anything older than seven years will eventually fall off.

Credit Bureaus = Your Teachers

In high school, your teachers were responsible for grading your work; in the world of credit, the credit bureaus are in charge of evaluating how you use your credit. Unlike your teachers, the credit bureaus are like invisible figures that grade all your credit moves whether you're aware of it or not. But trust me when I say they're there, and they know about that Target credit card . . . even if your significant other doesn't.

Of course, the most important player of all when it comes to your credit is you. You are in charge of how you manage your credit and how responsible you are with repayment. Like a small child, your credit needs your protection, attention, and care to make it grow and thrive. And did I mention patience? Chiiiile, you're going to need it, especially if your credit score is far from where you want it to be; it can take some time to increase it. But it can be done. Get good at doing the work and you'll be well on your way to accomplishing your credit score goal.

Score High (Credit) Step 1: Check Your Payment History (35% of Your Score)

Payment history is exactly what it sounds like—a record of how you've paid bills in the past. This includes whether they were paid on time and if you paid them in full or paid just the minimum amount. Accounting for 35% of your credit score, payment history is the most significant factor in your credit. This is likely because it's a good indicator of how you'll pay your bills in the future.

DO THE WORK ··························➤

Grab your credit report and get ready to act like a detective searching for discrepancies. I recommend focusing on the activity from the last two years, but consider digging as far back as four or five years. You want to make sure everything in the following areas looks accurate and, if it doesn't, make note of what's wrong.

Your personal information: This includes your name, address, and basic information.

This doesn't look right: _____

Any account information: Do all the accounts belong to you? Does your payment history appear to be accurate? You want to make sure, too, that any debts you've paid or accounts you've closed appear as such.

This doesn't look right: _____

Age of any negative history: Any late payments that are older than seven years should fall off your credit report. If anything beyond this age is still appearing on your report, you will want to request that it be removed (see the next page). Judgments, tax liens, and foreclosures can take up to ten years to fall off.

This doesn't look right: _____

If you've noted anything that doesn't look right, you will want to write a dispute letter. A dispute letter is formal correspondence that is sent to the credit bureaus indicating that there's an error on your credit report. You can find a form dispute letter at madewholeworkbook.com, but you can get started by collecting the relevant information below and transferring it over to your letter when you're ready. Once you have your letter finalized, it's best to send it via certified mail and ask for a return receipt.

And by the way, I know it's the twenty-first century and you might think it would be easier to complete a dispute letter online, but it continues to be best to have a good old-fashioned paper trail for your records.

Account number or other information to identify account: _____

Source of dispute information: _____
[Insert the name of the company, such as the bank, that provided the information to the credit reporting company.]

Type of disputed information: _____
[Insert public records information, unknown credit account/trade line, inquiry, etc.]

Dates associated with item being disputed: _____
[Insert the date that appears on your report.]

Explanation of item being disputed: _____
_____
[Insert details about why you think the information is inaccurate.]

IRL STORY: CARLA, LOS ANGELES, CA

When I was young and beginning my credit journey, I had to start from scratch because I didn't come from a family where you opened up credit to get things. My mom had messed up her credit at some point and just wouldn't touch credit cards, so it wasn't even a discussion.

When I did eventually get credit cards (when I was about eighteen), all I knew was that I should pay the bills. I didn't know the ins and outs of *credit*. It was through Tiffany's book and her group that I learned strategies for building and improving your credit: that you can call up the creditors and ask them to raise your credit; that you shouldn't have too many credit accounts, or let too many hard inquiries be pulled (what happens when you apply for credit or a loan). I also learned that you should keep your oldest credit card open because that assists with the length of your credit history. How long you've been using credit factors into your score, and if a credit card is closed, it's no longer adding to your history positively.

Over time, by applying these principles, I've seen my credit go from 700 to about 830—it's almost perfect. What I've found, though, is that improving your credit isn't just about applying principles; it can make your life better. When I applied to rent an apartment last year and my credit was run by the owners, they just kept saying I had an amazing score. I'm not one to try to prove something to people, but it made me feel good and like I was on the right track. It was a validation of my hard work and my dedication to being a good steward of my credit, and to my finances as a whole.

Having good credit has created *access*, and that's huge for me. I haven't needed a cosigner, I'm offered good interest rates, I don't have to put a deposit down on a rental car, I receive letters saying that my credit is being increased, I get the kinds of credit cards that give you perks. A lot of these things make my life a little easier and allow me to save money, all thanks to having good credit.

Eventually, I was able to add my mom onto one of my credit cards to have that trade line positively affect her score. I shared with her the tools and tips I learned from Tiffany, and she was able to build her credit. Little by little, she got her score up from 500 or so to 710. So now she's able to get a new car, and she's able to get a new credit card. That means this knowledge benefitted not only me but also helped my family and inner circle. It's just so influential.

Score High (Credit) Step 2: Reduce Your Amounts Owed and Improve Your Credit Utilization (30% of Your Score)

Credit utilization is the second most impactful factor on your credit score. This basically is a measure of how much of your available credit you have used. While your credit utilization score includes how you've used all types of credit, including credit cards, mortgages, and car loans, we are going to focus our discussion on credit card usage because it's the second most heavily weighted part of the score. The reason it gets more emphasis is because it's unsecured debt; that is, there's no asset for a bank to go after if you don't pay your bill. A mortgage or car loan is considered a secure debt because there is an asset (your home or vehicle) to back up the loan should you default.

The credit utilization part of your score is based on what percentage of your available credit is being used. For example, if you have $10,000 of available credit on your credit cards and you have used $5,000 of it, you are using 50% of your available credit. According to the credit bureaus, that's leaning on your credit a little too much. Generally, if you are using about 30% or less of your available credit, you are going to maximize this part of your credit score. And staying around 10% or lower can earn you even more points.

DO THE WORK ·····················➤

Your work in the area of credit utilization involves two steps: (1) calculating your current credit utilization percentage and (2) if needed, determining the best way to lower it.

1. Calculate Your Current Credit Utilization Percentage

Add up the credit limits on your credit card accounts. This includes store credit cards and bank-issued credit cards.

_____

_____

_____

_____

_____

Total: _____

Add up the balances on your accounts.

_____

_____

_____

_____

_____

Total: _____

Divide your balance by your credit limit and multiply the result by 100.

Balance _____ ÷ Credit limit _____ = _____ × 100 = _____

The number you get is the percentage of available credit you're using. If you want to try to lower it (which I advise if this number is above 30), move on to step 2.

2. Determine the Best Way to Lower Your Utilization Percentage

You can lower your credit utilization percentage either by paying down debt or increasing the amount of your credit limit. *Only increase your credit limit if you don't plan to use your card. Do not increase your limit if you are still actively using your card as this can present too much temptation to borrow money (remember that's what you are doing when you use credit!).*

Card(s) on which I can focus my debt paydown efforts:

Not sure? Use the Debt List you created in the debt chapter to get a sense of who you owe and how much.

Card description:

Card description:

Card(s) on which I can ask for an increase:

Card description:

Customer service number:

Card description:

Customer service number:

SHOULD I CLOSE MY CREDIT CARD?

If you're trying to clean up your house of (credit) cards, you might think it would be good to cancel some of your cards, but that's not always the best move. If you close a card, the credit limit from that account gets taken out of the utilization calculation, and this can bring your percentage up over 30%.

For example, let's say you have three cards with limits of $6,000, $4,000, and $2,000, giving you a combined limit of $12,000. And your balances on these accounts adds up to $3,000. Your current utilization calculation would be: 3,000 ÷ 12,000 = 0.25, or 25%. But if you were to close the account with a $6,000 limit, your utilization would be 3,000 ÷ 6,000 = 0.50, or 50%. In this case, closing the account could lower your credit score, and you'd likely be better off keeping the card.

To keep a card and use it responsibly, I recommend putting one or two smaller recurring charges on it and then paying it off each month after the statement date. This will let you get the "credit" for using credit well with the bureaus, and prevent the accumulation of additional debt.

Here are three questions to ask yourself when considering closing a card (circle either yes or no):

1. Do I still use it? YES/NO

2. Am I using it responsibly? YES/NO

3. Will it bring my utilization to over 30%? YES/NO

If you answer no to all three questions, it's likely you should close the card. If you answer yes to any, it's likely best to keep it.

Still feeling a little unsure? You can google "credit utilization calculator" to determine where you stand with your current balances and credit limits. Of course, you can also always visit the online tool kit to find some of my favorite free calculators.

Score High (Credit) Step 3: Identify the Length of Your Credit History/Hack Your Age (15% of Your Score)

Credit history (which accounts for 15% of your score) is the part of your credit score assigned based on how long you've used credit. Your oldest accounts and the average age of your open and closed accounts will be listed. Since this factor is really more about age than performance, it can seem to unfairly penalize people who have no or little credit history. But remember that a credit score is based on how you've used the credit available to you; without a history, it's really hard to have any kind of proof of performance.

The good news is that there are ways you can build your credit history (other than just sitting around and waiting for the years to pass). Here are a few of my favorite hacks:

Keep your oldest card. If you have already established your credit, be sure to keep your oldest card active and open. You can use the Jump Like Jordan method I mentioned in the Quick Start to do so.

Become an authorized user. If you don't have significant credit history, you can ask an individual you are close to if you can become an authorized user on one of their accounts. The key is, this person has to have excellent credit. Obviously, there are only a few people you can ask this favor of, since inquiring about someone's credit score can be touchy! You could probably ask your parents, siblings, or significant other . . . and maybe an aunt or uncle you're super close to.

When you become an authorized user on their credit card, you are "piggybacking" because you're essentially hitching a ride on their good credit. You don't get as much credit as when you are the primary user, but it does benefit your score in the long run.

It's important to understand that in this arrangement, you don't become responsible for the primary account holder's debt. But should the account go unpaid, it could lower your score because you're inheriting their behavior, good or bad, with the card.

On the flip side, if you're the one with the great credit, you can add an authorized user to your card in good standing. I did this for my not-so-baby sister, Lisa. It helped to raise her score, but her score didn't affect mine.

Get a credit-builder loan. This is what I call a fake-out loan. It's a loan, but you don't really get the money you borrow. What happens is a bank keeps the loaned money in an account for you while you make small payments over time. Once you pay off the fake-out loan, you actually get all your money back, plus interest if any has accrued in the savings account where your money was held.

I know it sounds a little confusing, but it's actually a great way for you to prove your ability to make payments and raise your credit score. The best part is that institutions that make these loans typically do not use your credit score (although they might consult ChexSystems, a verification service and consumer reporting agency that keeps track of bounced checks, unresolved overdrafts, and unpaid bank fees), and there are usually no up-front fees to get started.

Credit unions often have credit-builder loans, so if you're a member, be sure to ask. I share some of my favorite fake-out loan companies in the tool kit if you need recommendations.

Get a secured card. With a secured card, you put down a cash deposit and that is your credit limit, then you're issued a card that you're able to use like a regular (unsecured) credit card. It's called a secured card because your spending limit is secured with your deposit, and if you don't pay your bill, the bank will take what's owed from your deposit.

It might sound odd to give a lending institution, say, $1,000 only to be able to then spend that amount on a credit card. But if you establish a positive payment history on a secured card, you will likely see an increase in your credit score. And after six months to a year of good payment behavior, your deposit should be refunded, and you could be offered an unsecured (regular) card if the bank offers it. You can find secured card recommendations in the *Made Whole* tool kit.

DO THE WORK ·····················➤

1. Keep your oldest card open.
    Card description:
    Date card was opened:
    (Access this info from your credit report)

2. Become an authorized user.
    I will ask _____ if I can be an authorized user on their card. (Maybe bring their favorite refreshment to make this ask go over a little better!)

If you get an initial yes, here are some additional questions to ask:

Is it a positive account?

Does the card have a low balance and perfect payment history?

Is the card at least three years old?

Does the card issuer report authorized users to credit bureaus? (They can and should ask the issuer this question.)

Do you pay the card off in full each month?

You want all the answers to be yes in order for you to get the most out of being added as an authorized user.

If you don't feel comfortable asking these questions, you're probably not asking the right person. Be sure to make it clear that you don't want to use the card, and that you don't want the physical card or any kind of access at any point.

3. Get a credit-builder loan.

   Places I will inquire about a credit-builder loan:

   _____   _____

   _____   _____

4. Get a secured credit card.

   ☐ I will ask my bank if they offer a secured card.

What about cosigning for someone else, you ask? Don't! When you cosign, you aren't just vouching for the borrower, *you are also the borrower*. This means that if the person you are cosigning for does not pay, you are equally responsible for paying back that loan. The lender can sue you and come after you if the debt goes unpaid. Also, if you want to buy a home, the debt that you cosigned for can be included in your debt-to-income ratio (DTI), a number that banks use to see how much debt you already have so they can determine a cap on what they are willing to lend you. How terrible would it be to not qualify for your dream home because of a debt that's not really even yours? Sooo, if someone asks you to cosign, don't.

Score High (Credit) Step 4: Protect Your Credit Inquiries (10% of Your Score)

When you apply for credit, a company will run or "pull" your credit history to evaluate your score and creditworthiness. Your creditworthiness is a lender or creditor's assessment of how likely you are to pay your debts (it has nothing to do with your personal worth or value).

There are many scenarios that require a credit inquiry, including whenever you apply for a loan or credit card, or when you open a utility account or get a new cable or cell-phone plan.

When it's necessary, there's nothing wrong with having your credit run, but you want to be selective about who runs it and ensure that you know what type of inquiry is being done. There are two types of credit inquiries, referred to as soft and hard. It's important to know the difference as the actual act of running/pulling affects your credit differently.

A Soft Credit Inquiry (Also Known as a Soft Pull):

- Does not require your permission
- Does not impact your credit score at all
- Pulls partial information to see if you meet the most basic approval guidelines that a company has in place
- Can grant "prequalification" (credit card companies and lenders will run a soft pull on you before sending product offerings)

A Hard Credit Inquiry (Also Known as a Hard Pull):

- Requires your permission
- Impacts your credit score
- Asks for your Social Security number

Since hard inquiries have an impact on your credit score (they account for 10%) and require you to release more personal information, you want to be especially aware of how often you give permission for these to be run.

Credit Inquiry: Run It or Don't Run It?

Let Them Run It!	Don't Let Them Run It!
Mortgage—if you're buying, it's a must	Mortgage—for a preapproval only, ask if you can provide your own
Credit card—if it's going to benefit your financial health, such as by helping with utilization or getting you much-needed bonuses, like travel points	Credit card—if it's going to harm your financial health and/or if it's a store credit card
Utilities—do you want your lights on or not?	
Auto loan—yes, if it's mandatory, but ideally have it run through a credit union rather than the dealership; dealerships might run multiple hard pulls to try to approve you	
Applying for a rental property—yes, if it's mandatory	

DO THE WORK ·····················➤

You are fully in control and in charge of protecting yourself from credit inquiries. Take the pledge to protect your credit!

I, _____ [name], pledge not to open up a credit card unless it makes sense for my financial goals and overall financial wholeness health, because I know in the long run it's going to cost me more.

_____

[Signature]

It's not real unless you share on social. Tag me—I'm @thebudgetnista everywhere.

Score High (Credit) Step 5: Manage Your Credit Mix (10% of Your Score)

The last piece of your score is based on a factor referred to as credit mix. This is basically an assessment of how you do with various types of credit. Since it accounts for just 10% of your score, you can think of this bit of information as more of an FYI than an action item.

There are two types of credit: revolving credit and installment credit.

Revolving credit is your credit card because you pay it and that amount revolves, meaning that that available credit limit becomes available to you again.

Installment credit is when you get a loan and are required to make monthly installment payments until your loan is paid to zero and closed out.

There may be certain scenarios where a lender wants to see a mix regardless of your credit score, but generally it's not an issue and you can have an excellent score without having both kinds of credit. For example, I don't have installment loans, and my score is over 800.

DO THE WORK ·······················➤

Take a look at the types of credit you have to see what your mix looks like currently.

Revolving Credit

My credit cards:

_____   _____

_____   _____

Installment Loans

My installment loans:

_____   _____

_____   _____

How does your mix look? If you're lacking in one area, don't run out the door to go get yourself some fresh debt. But do take note of what type of credit you may be missing and know that adding this into the "mix" at some point might help your score climb just a little higher.

The Score High (Credit) Review

You are now ready to make your credit score climb by paying attention to the five factors that influence your score. These include payment history, credit utilization, length of credit history, credit inquiries, and credit mix. You know that wherever your score is currently, there are steps you can take to help increase it, and that with consistency, you will see your average trend upward, even if it takes time.

40% FINANCIALLY WHOLE

All right, you are nearly halfway to whole! I see you, and I acknowledge the work you are doing. Be sure you do the same. That's right—I want you to look at yourself in the mirror and say, "You're doing a good job. Yes, I'm talking to *you*." Sometimes you've just gotta show yourself some love!

CHAPTER 6

50% Whole

Learn to Earn
(Increase Your Income)

As I mentioned in chapter 2, there are two ways to increase the amount of money available to you—you can either spend less or make more. I find that people get stuck in the trying-to-spend-less space even when their efforts don't seem to pay off in a meaningful or truly noticeable way. And if you're already basically living on your Noodle Budget (see page 55), there's not much more you can save! In either of these cases, it's likely more productive to shift your efforts toward trying to earn more. And that's what this chapter is going to help you do—make more money.

If you jumped here from the budget chapter, you may have already diagnosed yourself as having a don't-make-enough issue, and you are eager to learn to earn. Even my spend-too-much-ers can benefit from the tools I'm going to share in the next few pages because hey, maybe, just maybe, you don't have to totally put the brakes on spending if you increase your earnings (but *please*, Sis: check in with the other components of financial wholeness before you spend away!).

My approach to increasing your take-home pay is about strategy, not suffering. I want to teach you how to earn more without sacrificing all your time or using up all your energy, because what good will extra money be if you're too tired to enjoy it? Life is too short to not live well now as you work toward creating a great life for later.

The Plan to Learn to Earn

Your mission here is to increase your income by maximizing what you are getting from your current job and/or tapping into your side-hustle skills. This isn't hard or complicated. You've just got to work your way through four simple steps:

1. Maximize your earning potential at your current job.
2. Assess your skills.
3. Decide which of these skills you can monetize.
4. Put a number on it: What's the income potential?

WHAT YOU'LL NEED

✓ Your résumé
✓ A LinkedIn account
✓ A brag book, aka a "Go me!" file

Quick Start

Not ready to do a deep dive into the upcoming steps just yet? No worries; here's a "simple and soon" action you can take now to help you start on your journey to making more: update your résumé and your LinkedIn profile. Sometimes we forget just how amazing we are and need to see it in black and white. LinkedIn is a great networking tool. If you've already got an account, make sure it's updated.

Learn to Earn Step 1: Maximize Your Earning Potential at Your Current Job

Here's a stat to startle you: According to a report from the staffing firm Randstad, 60% of women say they've never negotiated their salary. That means that waaay too many of us (like 60%!) take what we are offered and simply accept it. Say what?! That's a whole lot of potential earnings left on the table. So let's talk about how to collect *all* your coins at your current job first, before you seek out a side hustle.

There are essentially three ways to maximize your earnings potential at work. You can (1) ask for a raise because you think you should be earning more, (2) enhance or expand your skills so that asking for a raise is warranted by your employer's standards, and/or (3) maximize how much you make when you first get a job. I'll guide you through how to implement each of these strategies.

Ask for a Raise

It's common to overlook asking for a raise as the first and best way to make more money, but let's face it, if you're a woman in the majority I mentioned above, you probably aren't getting everything you deserve from your present employer. Not sure if you're getting shorted? Go online—I like the website Glassdoor, but Indeed and Payscale are good too—and see if you can find a national average for the specific job you do. How does your salary stack up against that average?

I know that the thought of asking for a raise makes a lot of people uncomfortable, and understandably so. Asking makes you feel vulnerable, and if the answer is no, you may feel disappointed and resentful. Hearing no can also increase your stress if you're relying on a raise to cover your increasing expenses. But if you can support your request for a raise, you will feel a whole lot less vulnerable—you'll feel better about yourself, and you'll know you deserve it—even if the company response is that they don't have more in the budget "at this time." The best way to support your request is to create what I call a brag book.

A brag book is a place, either a physical folder or notebook or a draft email or Google doc, where you document anything awesome you've done at work. The "wins" you want to keep track of will vary based on your job but could include any improvements you've made to the workflow, budget, or sense of community, and especially anything you've done to help save or make money for your company. Think of yourself as a director who's creating a highlight reel starring you—you want to draw attention to the things that make *you* shine! If the idea of "bragging" makes you squirm a little, call yours your "Go me!" file—that's the nickname my sister Tracy used for hers, and I love the burst of positive energy it adds to the list.

> **TIFFANY TIP:** When making a brag book, use numbers! How? Try your best to quantify your contributions to your workplace. How much money has each brag entry made or saved your company, directly or indirectly? Example: The new messaging system you implemented earned your employer $50,000 this year by helping them capture calls from interested customers. When you put a number on it, you're essentially not asking for a raise but for a salary correction based on all the measurable value you bring.

DO THE WORK ·······························➤

1. Go online and try to find the average salary for your job description or title. On Glassdoor, you can factor in your educational background and look at comparable salaries in your geographic region too. Got the number in mind now? Good; write it down.

   According to Glassdoor, the salary range for my current job is: _____.

   Use this number to help you gauge what you want to aim for.

2. Decide how you're going to document your accomplishments.

    I'm going to collect my accomplishments in a:

    ☐ Journal/notebook

    ☐ Google doc/draft email

    ☐ _____

    I'm going to name my collection:

    ☐ _____'s Brag Book

    ☐ Go Me!

    ☐ _____ (Craft your own title—your uniqueness is part of what makes you shine)

3. Start documenting!

    To help you get into the brag book mindset, think about some of the ways you've positively impacted your employer and/or place of employment and jot them down here:

    _____

    _____

    Don't forget to add the monetary value of that impact, if possible!

Enhance or Expand Your Skills

If you can't get an as-is increase in pay at your current job, you may be able to expand your skills as a way to enhance your value to your employer. This might mean taking classes or seeking a professional designation or certificate. But before you dust off your backpack, remember that your goal is to increase your income rather than increase your spending, so you'll want to see if your company will cover the cost of any training or education before you pay for it out of pocket. If it's not something your company will pay for, do a little more digging to make sure your personal investment will generate some type of return, even if it's in a different role or with a different employer. You should also talk to other people in the position you're aiming for and ask if they received the same training and if it proved beneficial. And if not, what type of training did they get? Some people will be more forthcoming than others with this kind of information; it might help to point out that you're not coming after their job (at least not yet!).

DO THE WORK ·······················➤

In order for me to get the pay increase or job I want, I need the following items:

_____

_____

I'm going to ask _____ what kind of training or education they received to get their job. The training/certificate/education they recommended was:

_____

_____

Maximize How Much You Make When You First Get a Job

If you are searching and interviewing for primary employment, you have the opportunity to try to make the most you can from the very beginning. One of the worst things you can do is make less money than you should be making out of the gate. If this happens, you inadvertently establish an earnings gap that you then have to work doubly hard to bridge, even if you seek employment elsewhere later. This is because many prospective employers will ask what you made before and use that to determine what to offer you.

DO THE WORK ·····················➤

Visit Glassdoor.com, Indeed.com, and Payscale.com to get a sense of the salary range you're working with. My research has revealed that the salary range is:

_____.

☐ I've gotten super clear on the salary range for my desired job.

Rehearse what to say. A huge part of maximizing how much you make is knowing what to say (and what not to say) when you're in the negotiating phase. I've consulted my amazing *Brown Ambition* podcast cohost, Mandi Woodruff-Santos, for some tips you can use when you're talking salary. Mandi is a career and negotiation expert who has helped thousands of women learn to earn what they deserve. Here are some scripts she shared from her Nail the Negotiation course:

If You Want More Base Compensation:
YOU SAY: "Is there room to bump up the base compensation? I would feel more comfortable with an increase of $_____."

If You Fear You Lowballed Yourself:
YOU SAY: "I'd like to revisit the base salary. Given the scope of the role and duties that I've learned about through the interview process, I would feel more comfortable if you could increase the base salary to $_____."

If They Say, "But This Was the Range You Gave Us Before":
YOU SAY: "I understand completely. As I stated at the time, it was a range that I offered prior to fully understanding the scope of the role. Given the discussions I've had since that point, I believe a salary of $_____ is in better alignment for me."

If You're Weighing Other Job Offers and Need Time:
YOU SAY: "I want to be transparent that I'm weighing another offer at this time. I'm expecting it to come through in ___ day(s). Could you give me ___ hours to reflect on the offers and get back to you?"

☐ I've reviewed the scripts and will rehearse them before my next interview!

Learn to Earn Step 2: Assess Your Skills

If you feel you've maximized your earning potential at your job and still need additional income, it's time to identify your best options for a side hustle. While this might sound like something that could be figured out by a quick "best side-hustle gigs" online search, you can find more specific results and will likely be more successful if you do the work in this chapter. I'm gonna show you how.

To find the side hustle that's best for you, you want to first take an inventory of your existing skills; actually having to write them down can be eye-opening, believe me. You're likely going to find that you're good at more than you thought! This self-inventory isn't always easy to take, but I have some tricks to help you.

DO THE WORK ·······················➤

Use these prompts to begin identifying your skills.

- What do I find myself doing in my free time?

_____

_____

- What do people come to me regularly for?

_____

_____

- What comes to me easily?

_____

_____

- What did I want to be when I was little? (Not sure? Ask your parent or a close relative if you mentioned any life aspirations before the age of ten.)

_____

_____

Now write down some of your skills. If you're still not sure, start to pay attention to when people ask you a favor and make note of this.

You can also go one step further and be proactive about asking others to help you with this; others often see us better than we see ourselves. Maybe you could ask a friend, family member, or coworker. Simply say, "I want to know—what would you say I'm good at?" (Maybe don't ask the sibling who's most likely to answer with "Annoying your sibling" or "Not returning the clothes you borrow." You know the sibling I'm talking about!)

What I think I'm good at:

_____

_____

_____

_____

_____

What other people think I'm good at:

_____

_____

_____

_____

_____

IRL STORY: NATASHA, BOSTON, MA

I've always been a multiple streams kind of person, and most recently I had a side hustle as a courier making Amazon deliveries. This meant waking up at 3:00 a.m., putting wear and tear on my car, and spending money on gas and oil changes and maintenance. I thought I was earning extra money, but when Tiffany pointed out that your side hustle shouldn't cost you more than you are making, I realized that I hadn't really done that math. When I did, I discovered that what I was making was being put back into the expenses related to the job. It wasn't worth it!

So I ended up finding another side hustle teaching fitness classes through an online module. My primary job is managing a fitness facility remotely, and my interest in fitness means I have my own equipment at home, so it aligns much better. Since it leans into my passion a bit more, I feel more fulfilled. I'm moving my body; I'm connecting with other people and making money at the same time. Plus, I'm happier, and since I was doing the delivery stuff during all kinds of early-morning and late-night hours, I'm also safer and getting more sleep.

Of course, the other bonus is that I'm able to save more. I'm even doing the automated savings that Tiffany recommends! I can now say, "OK, *this* is the extra cushion from a side hustle that I wanted."

I'm also a big fan of the brag book. I use a list-making app called Trello to keep track of my accomplishments at work. I have my work broken into different areas, and each time I finish something, I move it to Completed. When it came time to negotiate for a raise, I had this entire list of completed tasks, and they were dated and neatly organized. My bosses were able to say, "She's been here for less than a year and she's completed all these tasks and done all these things to improve our program." This helped me get a 4% raise!

Learn to Earn Step 3: Decide Which of These Skills You Can Monetize

Once you have a good sense of your skills, it's time to figure out which might translate into an income-earning side hustle. Let's say you're an engineer with culinary chops—might you be able to put those cooking skills to use to make money? Maybe you could act as sous chef for a private chef as a side gig. Remember, though, this effort isn't about nurturing a new hobby; you're looking for income. Also, keep in mind that not every skill will help you bring in more money, and yet some skills may bring in more than you think. That's why I want you to investigate before you invest time, money, or energy; research will help prevent the wasting of any of these valuable things.

To help best determine which skills of yours you'll want to focus on, work through these next three baby steps:

1. Consider Your Current Skill Set First

It usually makes the most sense to first consider the skills you already use in your primary job. This doesn't require learning a whole new skill set; it simply has you double-dip into the one you already have to start earning extra cash. Here are some examples of how this could work:

- Keisha, an HR specialist, helped people develop résumés and prepare for job interviews.
- Renée, an accountant, started bookkeeping for small businesses.
- Lisa, a biochemist, offered consulting services related to her expertise.
- Tiffany (that's me!), a teacher, babysat and tutored within her community.

DO THE WORK: CAN YOU GIG IT? ·····················➤

Open up a browser and type in your primary job—"teacher," "bookkeeper," "Realtor," "writer"—and see what kind of side jobs pop up. Write down any ideas you find.

My current primary job:

_____

_____

Potential side-hustle ideas found in my search:

_____

_____

2. Supercharge Your Current Skill Set

If you want to make the largest amount of money out of your side hustle, it's smart to embellish your established wheelhouse before starting to build a whole new one. This means looking for ways to enhance your expertise in an area that you already went to school for or in which you have a degree or certification.

To use myself as an example again, I eventually got my master's in education, which allowed me to both make more as a teacher and increase my tutoring fee; in fact, I was able to command twice as much as tutors who didn't have their master's.

That said, before you go and spend money on any training program or additional education, make sure the math works. Ask yourself some questions, such as: "Does it make more sense to put this money toward retirement or toward paying down debt? Or will using it to gain a skill set allow me to make more in the long run?" Bust out that calculator and see where you'll get the biggest return on your investment.

3. Set Limits on Your Investment into Seedling Skills

Some skills will need nurturing before they bear the fruit of side-hustle income. These are the kind of skills you will need to spend some money to acquire before they can make you money. For example, you might need to take some public speaking classes so you're better able to teach your expertise. Or it could benefit you to learn to do basic graphic design so you can create a workbook to sell to organizations that hire you to consult. Investing in yourself in these kinds of ways can be financially productive, but you always want to keep your main objective—earning more—in mind.

One way to stay focused on earning more is to make sure there's a direct return on any money you put into a side hustle. An indirect return is only okay after you have enough money to wait out getting money back from that investment. (BTW, there's nothing wrong with an indirect return if you're starting a business, but if you want to make money now, it may not be worth it.)

Let me use my friend Rehana to demonstrate what I mean by "direct" and "indirect" returns. Reh is an amazing interior designer who had two part-time jobs in her field and occasionally did smaller consulting jobs on the side. She even designed my beautiful homes! After a while, she wanted to go out on her own, but she wasn't sure how much she wanted to invest in the switch.

Rehana had to consider her potential return on investment (ROI), specifically whether items purchased would provide a direct or indirect return.

Direct ROI Item: Design software. She needed this software to create digital layouts for her potential new clients because she understood that the right software could cut down her work by hours a day.

Indirect ROI Items: Business cards, flyers, a website; items that could ultimately garner her business but weren't tied directly to her completing a job.

Here are some other examples of direct versus indirect ROI items.

NAME: SHEILA
SIDE HUSTLE: BAKING CAKES

Direct ROI Items:	Indirect ROI Items:
Cake-making ingredients (flour, sugar, eggs, baking powder, etc.) and cake-packaging materials (boxes)	Business cards, flyers, a website, and maybe even a larger oven one day

NAME: MELISSA
SIDE HUSTLE: PERSONAL TRAINING

Direct ROI Items:	Indirect ROI Items:
Basic weight set, jump rope, and exercise mats to use to train clients in her backyard or spare room	Ads in the local paper, rented gym space

You don't have to get too bogged down in these details if you do one thing: Focus on the money. Do not put so much money into a side hustle that it can come back to sink you, meaning don't take out loans or max out credit card balances. Avoid spending on things that you won't essentially get a refund on when you get paid for your work, and you'll be good.

DO THE WORK ·····················➤

Carry over your skills from your "what I think I'm good at" and "what other people think I'm good at" lists, and do some research to help you complete the added columns.

Skill set	Can it be monetized within my current life? Y/N	Will it yield a direct return? Y/N

Learn to Earn Step 4: Put a Number on It. What's the Income Potential?

Once you've figured out which of your skills can be monetized, you want to get a sense of how much your side gig can realistically bring in each month. Ask yourself how much you think you can make, and if you're not sure, look up people who are offering the service you want to provide and see what they are charging. Use their rates as a guide to help put yourself in the ballpark. Keep in mind that you'll want to find a comparable rate in your area, if possible, as pricing for most things varies regionally.

> **TIFFANY TIP:** If three or more people say yes quickly to your rates, it's likely time to raise your prices. If your services are priced right, you should actually encounter a little market resistance at first, and then acceptance once people start to spread the word that your work is worth it.

Once you put your side-hustle skills out into the marketplace, keep an open mind about how the experience is going to go and how it could impact your future. A side hustle can be like a shape-shifter; it might start out as one thing and evolve into something totally different.

In my friend Rehana's case, she had her master's in design, was a part-time professor of architecture and design at a college, and had a part-time job at Lowe's as an in-house designer. Working as a part-time professor wasn't paying much, and she wanted to maximize her time. She decided to try her hand at working with individual design clients. She was my neighbor, and I got to be her first client. She leveraged the power of social media to showcase her work and attract more clients while working on my home, and two years in, she was able to quit her other jobs. Her side hustle became her main hustle.

Now, this doesn't mean your experience will mirror Rehana's, but I share it to show you the potential that exists in the side-gig space. You never know what can happen when you put yourself out there!

DO THE WORK ·······················➤

Use this chart to help document how much money your skill set could earn each month.

Skill set	Can it be monetized within my current life? Y/N	Will it yield a direct return? Y/N	Monthly income potential

It wouldn't feel right to Teacher Tiffany to move on without having you set a date to start earning. Let's make it real.

I will start monetizing my _____ [insert skill set] on _____ [insert date].

Share your commitment with me on social; I'm @thebudgetnista everywhere.

The Learn to Earn Review

You now know the learn-to-earn drill: spot your skills and monetize them to help pay your bills (or stock your savings, but that didn't rhyme!). Focus first on the most efficient path to increasing your monthly income by trying to make more money at your current job. Then look to your current skill set to see if there are ways you can enhance your education or expertise there. If you have to put some money into your side hustle, make sure it's funds that will come right back to you when you get paid.

50% FINANCIALLY WHOLE

Big news: You are 50% financially whole! Go you. For real—this is life-improving stuff.

CHAPTER 7

60% Whole
Invest Like an Insider
(Retirement and Wealth)

In this chapter, I'm going to help you get good with two types of investing: investing for retirement and investing for wealth building. While both can offer something priceless—peace of mind when it comes to money—the goals of each are distinctly different.

With investing for retirement, the goal is to save and grow your money to an amount that will allow you to maintain your current lifestyle even after you stop working. You do this because you want to live comfortably later on without worrying that you'll have to work forever. You accomplish this by creating and implementing your investment plans with the help of your human resources representative, a certified financial planner (CFP), or online tools, or by yourself.

With investing for wealth, the goal is to upgrade your life in the present (which will also help in the future, of course), and also possibly to leave a legacy. You accomplish this through consistent contributions toward investing, and by learning to leave your invested money alone to give it the opportunity to grow.

Investing for Retirement

The Plan for Investing for Retirement

To take care of your future self, you will need to invest consistently and automatically into a retirement account. Here are the four steps necessary to get started:

1. Determine how much you need to save for retirement.
2. Decide where to put your money.
3. Choose your investment mix/asset allocation.
4. Set up automation and limit your withdrawals and loans as much as humanly possible.

Quick Start: Invest in a Transfer Date Fund (TDF)

Words to live by: The older you get, the less risky your retirement investments should get. After all, you don't want to risk losing a lot of money when you're about to cash in your account to live on in retirement. One of the reasons you may be hesitant about investing for retirement is that you're not sure how much to put where. But what if I told you there was a tool that would figure out your investment allocation mix for you? And that it was automated. It's a mutual fund, and it's called a target date fund.

A target date fund is an age-based retirement investment that helps you to take more risks when you're young and fewer when you're older. The fund will automatically rebalance itself year after year in order to make sure the closer you get to your target, the more conservative your investments. The target date is the year you plan on retiring.

Take a look at the investment choices in your retirement account and see if TDFs are offered. Ideally, you want to choose one that follows the overall stock

> market, since the market has returned an average yield of 10% in the last 100 years. And you want to choose the dates closest to your desired retirement day.

WHAT YOU'LL NEED

- ✓ A sense of the year you want to retire
- ✓ An idea of how much you want to live on per year during retirement
- ✓ Your imagination—so you can create an awesome retirement in your mind before creating a plan to reach it
- ✓ Access to your current retirement account(s) and/or the company you think you'll use to open a new one

> **TIFFANY TIP:** It's your younger self's job to look after your older self. Keep in mind that one day you may not want to or even be able to work. What do you need to do now so you can look after that version of you?

Investing for Retirement Step 1: Determine How Much You Need to Save for Retirement

How much money you need for retirement—your retirement goal—depends on a few factors, such as how soon you hope to retire and what you expect your lifestyle to look like when you reach retirement age. Figuring this out first will help you create a plan that will bring your retirement vison to life down the road. Keep in mind that early retirement is considered to be fifty-five years old or younger, and traditional retirement age is mid-sixties, specifically sixty-five and older.

Your Retirement Goal

If you want to retire early or earlier than early, there are a few different ways you can figure out your future savings:

- **Multiply your annual expenses by 25.** A person with 25 times their annual expenses invested for retirement will likely never run out of money when retired if they withdraw 4% or less from their retirement account to live on each year. This is because the market rate of return (the amount earned on money invested in the stock market) over the last thirty years has been around 10%, which is obviously well over the 4% you'll be using.

  Sample Calculation: $50,000 (expenses) × 25 (years in retirement if you retire by sixty-five) = $1,250,000 (how much you need to have in your retirement account by age sixty-five)

- **Multiply your annual income/take-home pay (instead of your annual expenses) by 25.** Saving this amount will provide a bigger buffer during retirement, but it will take longer to reach this goal.

  Sample Calculation: $85,000 (annual income/take-home pay) × 25 (years in retirement if you retire by sixty-five) = $2,125,000 (how much you need to have in your retirement account by age sixty-five)

- **Multiply your current annual expenses by 30 and save aggressively—up to 70% of your income—to achieve this savings goal as quickly as possible.** This aggressive saving strategy was introduced in a book called *Your Money or Your Life* by Vicki Robin and Joe Dominguez and is aligned with the FIRE movement. FIRE stands for Financial Independence, Retire Early. True FIRE followers save *and* invest aggressively with the goal of retiring early.

  Sample Calculation: $35,000 (annual expenses if you live super simply and on your Noodle Budget) × 30 (extra years in retirement if you want to retire early) = $1,050,000 (how much you need to retire the FIRE way; you'd retire early but would have to live simply during retirement too)

If you want to retire at the traditional age or later, or without as much of a cushion, use this calculation to determine your financial needs:

- **Multiply your annual salary by 12.** At first glance, you might think this number would fall short of supporting you deep into retirement (assuming, God willing, it lasts more than twelve years). But there are ways you can make this amount work, such as by sticking strictly to living off no more than 4% of your earnings; reinvesting anything you make beyond the 4%; and retiring later in life so you get the maximum Social Security benefits. It's worth noting that most people are able to live off 75 to 80% of their preretirement financial needs thanks to declining expenses during post-work life.

    Sample Calculation: $100,000 (annual gross salary) × 12 (years in retirement if you're okay with retiring later) = $1,200,000 (amount you need to save and grow to by your later retirement age)

You might be wondering how you're going to get to these big numbers. Well, you're not going to do it via saving alone. You are going to take advantage of a little miracle called compound interest. Compound interest is when your money is making you money and the money your money made (interest) is making you money.

The best part about compound interest is that the only thing you need to do to start accumulating it is to get your money into an interest-earning savings account, and then let the magic happen (although an interest-earning savings account alone won't earn you enough to retire, you'll have to eventually put your money to work by investing). In the beginning, your invested funds might not look like they are growing, but stay the course. Compound interest is kind of like a slow cooker, and this is the recipe for a tasty retirement: Deposit plenty of cash, season it with an automated investment strategy, cook for a heap of time, and enjoy.

The key to getting the most out of compound interest is time. The sooner you put your money into a retirement account, the sooner it can start growing. And like when using a slow cooker, don't even think about lifting the lid to sneak a bite before the cooking is done. You put your cash under that lid, and you leave it alone and allow it to marinate and stew.

Your Contribution Amount

Now it's time to figure out how much or what percentage of your income you need to contribute monthly to your retirement account to get to your goal.

There are limits to how much you can contribute to a retirement account (see below), but in the ideal scenario, you are contributing 20% or more of your income toward your retirement. To put it in numbers, if you make $60,000 a year, you would contribute $12,000 a year, or $1,000 a month. I'll wait while you gasp a little . . . I know it sounds like *a lot*. OK, now take a deep breath because the good news is that there are strategies that can help you get there, and you can get there over time. Most people can't just go all high-rolling retirement investor right out of the gate—they have to start at a lower percentage and work their way up. I'll help you get to your max.

Hacks to Help You Get to 20%

Collect on your employer's match and/or profit-share program. If your company offers a 401(k) or 403(b) retirement account, be sure to ask if they offer a match on any contributions you make into these accounts. An employer match, aka free money, is a payment to your retirement account based on a percentage of your annual gross income (your pay before taxes and deductions). A company match can range from 1% to 10% or higher (rare).

To give you an example of how this works, let's say your annual income is $50,000 and your retirement benefits include a 4% match. In money terms, this would mean your employer will contribute up to $2,000 per year into your retirement account.

You will want to check if there are conditions you have to meet to get the match. These might include needing to have worked at your job for a certain period of time or to have put in an equal percentage as your company. No matter what the conditions are, you want to do your best to meet them and secure this free money!

Some companies may offer a profit-share contribution instead of a match. This type of contribution is unlikely to have conditions that you need to meet but may be dependent upon the company's profits each year; that is, little to no profits likely means little to no profits to share.

How It Can Help: Any contribution made by your company helps boost your retirement account balance, plus it counts toward your 20% goal. That is, if they put in 4%, your goal requirement drops to 16%. If they put in 5%, your contribution drops to 15%, and so on. If you get a profit share, the amount is less predictable, so you'll want to plan on funding your plan fully until your employer lets you know how much they will contribute based on the year's performance.

Increase your savings rate by making more. How much you earn minus how much you spend will give you a percentage known as your savings rate. If you earn $3,000 and you spend $2,000, you have $1,000 leftover for savings, a savings rate of 33%. The higher your savings rate, the greater the amount of funds that can be directed right into your retirement account.

In chapter 2, I mentioned the two ways to increase your savings rate: (1) earn more and (2) spend less. With your retirement goal in mind, lean hard but smart into your efforts to earn more. Begin with the easiest way to increase your income by asking for a raise. Far too few people approach their employer with a supported ask (see chapter 6 for how to build and present your case for a raise), and they end up leaving money on the table. It's time to go in with your brag book in hand and ask for a pay increase.

How It Can Help: When you boost your savings rate, you give yourself the opportunity to save more for retirement, which will help you capitalize more fully on compound interest.

Invest a lower annual percentage of your income for retirement. It's true that saving 20% of your income for retirement is the ultimate goal. But the reality is that not everyone will be able to contribute that much now or even ever; if you have to start at 1%, it's a start that gives you something to build on. Just be sure that you keep working toward 20% so that you can make the most of investment growth and compound interest.

How It Can Help: As the poet Julia Abigail Fletcher Carney said, "Little drops of water make the mighty ocean." In other words, what might feel like just a drop in your retirement bucket can go on to become something much bigger if you give it a chance.

When choosing an employer, consider the retirement package being offered. Most people compare job opportunities based on salary and schedule, but I recommend that retirement benefits get moved near the top of your list of considerations when on a job search. Some retirement benefits may become effective only after a probationary term of employment is met; this is something you want to keep in mind as you explore employment options.

How It Can Help: Some employers offer a very generous match or profit share, and these contributions can be all you need to bridge the gap between where you are with your retirement contribution and your goal of 20%.

DO THE WORK ·····················➤

Calculate Your Retirement Goal

If you are aiming for early retirement, use one of these calculations to provide your goal amount:

Multiply your annual expenses by 25.

_____ [current annual expenses] × 25 = _____

Multiply your annual income by 25.

_____ [current annual income] × 25 = _____

Multiply your current annual expenses by 30.

_____ [current annual expenses] × 30 = _____

If you are aiming for a traditional retirement age, use this calculation to provide your goal amount:

Multiply your annual income by 12.

_____ [current annual income] × 12 = _____

Calculate Your Contribution Amount

Calculate the percentage of your income you need to set aside in your retirement account annually (then monthly) to reach your goal. Remember to include the money you will personally invest, as well as the money you can invest with the help of your employer's match or contribution (if applicable).

In the _Made Whole_ online tool kit (madewholeworkbook.com), I've included a handy calculator to help you identify how many years of savings and investing it will take you to be fully ready to retire—you'll just plug in your numbers, and I'll do the math!

Use the calculator to help you identify how many years of savings and investing it will take you to be fully ready to retire.

IRL STORY: ERICA, CHICAGO, IL

During the pandemic, I started looking at where I was in terms of retirement and how much more time I wanted to devote to my current employment. I had been working for the city of Chicago for twenty-three years, and my eligibility for retirement was about four years away. But as far as I could tell, I was pretty far away from having things in order to be able to retire then. It created a lot of anxiety for me.

Then I picked up Tiffany's _Get Good with Money_ and started working my way through the retirement chapter. The first thing I did was calculate my expenses for a year and multiply that by 25 to get my retirement goal. Next, I did some division to see what my monthly contribution needed to be to reach this goal. This quick bit of math revealed to me that I needed to increase my contributions by nearly $1,000 a month to meet my retirement needs. Let me tell you—that number was daunting to see on paper.

I initially didn't feel like I could achieve such an increase in contributions. But I kept reading Tiffany's advice to just "start where you are" and "do what you can," and it was a really encouraging confidence booster. So I looked at ways to boost my income and/or reduce some expenses to increase my contributions. I started selling Mary Kay products, and I'm also an author, so I began offering consulting services to help other writers with their process. This increased the amount I was able to contribute to my retirement. I also made some shifts in where exactly my retirement contributions were going.

After almost two years of following some of the retirement strategies Tiffany introduced me to, I am able to invest an additional $1,000 a month into my retirement. It has taken some sacrifice, but it was really about a mindset shift for me. I am now actively engaged in the process of creating my future. And while I am currently only about 30% of the way to my goal, I am positioned to hit about 85% of my goal by the time I actually want to retire. I never thought that would be possible.

Investing for Retirement Step 2: Decide Where to Put Your Money

Now it's time to discuss where you might put your retirement savings. In general, there are four different accounts that will suit most people.

1. 401(k)

If you work for a for-profit company or corporation, your employer may offer you access to a type of investment account called a 401(k) or 403(b). The account will be referred to as a 403(b) if you work for a nonprofit, a school, or the government. (For simplicity's sake, I'm going to refer to it as a 401(k) throughout this section, but know that I'm referring to both.) 401(k)s have some real advantages:

- **They are pre-taxed contributions.** You won't pay taxes on money you put into a 401(k), which means more money invested now. But note that you will pay taxes when you pull it out during retirement.
- **They help lower your annual income taxes.** If you make $50,000 a year and you put $5,000 in your 401(k), you'll be taxed on $45,000 instead of $50,000.
- **They have high contribution limits.** As of this writing, people under fifty can put in $22,500 a year into their 401(k)s; people over fifty can put in an additional $7,500 in catch-up contributions, for a total of $30,000. And your employer can contribute up to $43,500 on your behalf for a total max contribution allowance of $66,000 if you're under fifty and $73,500 if you're fifty or older.
- **They offer a set "menu" of investing options.** This is great if you just want your money to be managed without requiring you to make many decisions. If you want more say in how your funds are invested, you may want to check out an IRA as well.

2. Traditional IRA

An IRA is an individual retirement account. When you put your money into an IRA, you have more choice over where your money gets invested. IRAs also have some real advantages:

- **They allow pre-taxed contributions.** You will pay taxes on the money you put into a traditional IRA (including earnings and gains) only when you withdraw it.
- **They are a 401(k) rollover option.** If you leave a job, you can roll your 401(k) funds into an IRA.
- **They help lower your income taxes.** Your contributions, up to a certain amount, are tax deductible in the year you make them.

3. Roth IRA

A Roth is another type of IRA, but it has some significant differences from the traditional version:

- **You pay taxes before you invest your money in a Roth.** The plus side of this is that you pay today's tax rate instead of an unknown future rate upon withdrawal. Once you are ready to use your funds in retirement, you can start drawing on them (including your earnings and gains) tax-free. One exception—if you withdraw money from your Roth before the age of fifty-nine and a half and before the account is five years old, you'll have to pay taxes and penalties on any growth in the account.
- **There are no required withdrawals by a certain age.** Most other types of retirement accounts require you to pay penalties if you don't start withdrawing funds by age seventy-two. But a Roth can continue to grow and, if you don't end up having a need for it, be left to your heirs.
- **They have an income limit.** A Roth IRA is not an investment option if you make more than a certain amount of money. The current income caps are $153,000 for an individual and $228,000 for married couples filing jointly. These limits are updated annually, so please do a search for your current year. There *are* ways around these limits with something called a "backdoor Roth IRA," a type of conversion that allows folks with high incomes to fund a Roth despite IRS income limits. Basically, you put money you've already paid taxes on in a traditional IRA, then convert your contributed funds into a Roth IRA. You definitely want to consult with your financial adviser before doing this.

4. SEP IRA

If you're self-employed or work for a company that doesn't offer a 401(k), you can put money into a simplified employee pension, or SEP. You may have access to this type of account via your employer if you work for a small company, or you can set one up for yourself. Some features of a SEP IRA:

- **They allow pre-tax contributions.** Similar to a 401(k) or traditional IRA contribution, your SEP contribution is made pre-tax.
- **They help lower your income taxes.** You can deduct 25% of your income or currently up to $66,000 per year, whichever is the lesser value. As with other investment vehicles, you will want to check SEP contribution limits each year as the IRS updates them annually.

Spot Your Retirement Self

So, now that you have the information on the various types of retirement accounts, you may be thinking, *OK, OK... but what's the* action, *Tiffany? Help a girl out!* I've got you covered. Let's look at a few IRL investing-for-retirement scenarios. Find yourself in one of these scenarios and consider the next best steps as laid out.

Scenario 1: *You have access to a 401(k), and your employer offers a match.* Ideally, you want to start by investing for retirement with your 401(k) up to the match. Then move on to maxing out your Roth. If you still have funds available, contribute up to the max of your 401(k).

Scenario 2: *You have access to a 401(k), but your employer does not offer a match.* Max out your Roth IRA first, and then start working on maxing out the 401(k).

Scenario 3: *You have access to a SEP.* I would probably still max out the Roth IRA first, then work toward maxing out the SEP.

Scenario 4: *You don't have access to a 401(k) or a SEP.* This can occur if you work for a small company or a start-up that doesn't offer a 401(k) and/or you're not self-employed.

Unfortunately, you don't have many options in this case. I would max out a Roth IRA, then create a taxable investment account to start putting away money for retirement. Though you don't get the tax-deferred growth and will pay tax on the account each year, you will still be saving for retirement, and that's a powerful thing to do.

DO THE WORK ·······················➤

You have been briefed on the most common retirement account options. Now it's time to decide into which type of account you want to direct your funds.

If you work for a company, the government, or a nonprofit, take the following steps:

1. Contact your HR department to ask about the specific 401(k) or 403(b) plans available to you.
2. Start with a target date fund. Automate the withdrawals from your paycheck, and make sure to do the math so you don't overcontribute. Example: If you get twenty-six checks annually and you start contributing in January and are single, your max contribution is $22,500. Divide that by twenty-six checks and you'll know the maximum amount you should have come out of your check. $22,500 ÷ 26 = $865 per check.

If you are self-employed, take the following steps:

1. Connect with a brokerage firm to find out how to set up a SEP IRA. A financial adviser can help you with this too. Use chapter 10 to help you find an adviser, and also visit the tool kit to see some of my top brokerage picks.
2. Ask if they offer a Roth IRA as well.

No matter whom you work for, be sure to think about whom your beneficiary will be. A beneficiary is the person or persons who will receive the money in your accounts if you pass away. You'll be asked to name a beneficiary when you sign up for a plan. I'll talk all about this in the insurance chapter.

My Retirement Accounts Will Include:

(Check all that apply)

☐   A 401(k)

☐   A traditional IRA

☐   A Roth IRA

☐   A SEP

My Beneficiaries Will Be:

You can keep this info to yourself if you'd prefer . . . or write here "Whoever starts doing all the dishes and taking out the trash" and leave it out on the kitchen table to see if anyone is paying attention.

_____

Investing for Retirement Step 3: Choose Your Investment Mix/Asset Allocation

When you put your money into a retirement account, it's usually invested in at least a couple different types of investments. Your funds might be put into a few stocks and a lot of bonds, or vice versa. What do these terms really mean? See page 158 for more detailed definitions, but for now what's important is to know the simplified versions:

A stock is a portion of or piece of ownership in a company. Stocks can go up and down in value quickly as they are driven by unpredictable economic factors.

A bond is an investment in a loan to a company or a state. Bonds are more stable as they are basically a loan that earns interest. With stability, though, comes less opportunity for growth.

Mutual funds are a collection of stocks, bonds, and other securities (a security is a financial asset that can be bought, sold, or traded). If you invest in a mutual fund, you are buying stocks with other people, which is why it's called "mutual."

An exchange-traded fund (ETF) is a mash-up of a mutual fund and a stock. Like a mutual fund, it's a basket of different types of investments, and like a stock, it can be traded on the public exchange on weekdays within the trading hours of 9:30 a.m. to 4:00 p.m. Eastern Standard Time. Mutual funds trade only once per day after the market closes.

Index funds are also collections of stocks, but the stocks are invested in a compilation of specific companies that make up an index. These indexes include the S&P 500, the Dow Jones Industrial Average, and the Nasdaq Composite (these names probably all sound familiar).

This divvying up or diversification is referred to as your investment mix (also called asset allocation). Understanding your investment mix is important because it's basically the easiest way to manage your risk with your retirement money.

While there are several ways to allocate your assets, I focus on determining your investment risk based on how much you have in stocks versus how much in bonds. Generally, you want to be invested in both as stocks can give you momentum in growing your investment, and bonds can provide a slow and steady form of growth.

There are a handful of factors that can play into figuring out what percentage of each you want to have your money in—your tolerance for risk and your base income, for starters. However, one simple and smart way to split your selections is to focus on another factor: your age. Remember that the closer you get to retirement, the less risk you want to take with the money you're soon going to be relying on when you're not working. So, as you age, your percentage in stocks should go down because they are riskier, and your percentage in bonds should go up as they are less risky.

I love using what's commonly called the rule of 110 to figure out the right percentage: You subtract your age from 110 and use the bigger number as your stock percentage and the smaller number as your bond percentage.

For example, if you're thirty-five, that's 110 − 35 = 75. That means you should invest 75% in stocks and 25% in bonds. Next year, when you're thirty-six, your percentages would be 74% stocks and 26% bonds, and so on.

DO THE WORK ·····················➤

Calculate your investment mix using the rule of 110.

110 − _____ age = _____

Percentage of retirement funds to be invested in stocks = _____

Percentage of retirement funds to be invested in bonds = _____

Investing for Retirement Step 4: Set Up Automation and Limit Your Withdrawals and Loans as Much as Humanly Possible

I will never stop preaching the goodness and glory of automation! It helps us pay our bills on time every time, and also budget and save without even thinking. And it's going to help you start or continue building your retirement fund without requiring extra work from you. All you have to do is confirm your monthly contribution amount (from step 1 on page 131) and set up the automatic transfer into your account. If you work for an employer, you can likely set this up through your payroll department. If you manage your own retirement accounts, you typically can set up automatic transfers through your bank into an external brokerage account.

Now, one thing that can't be automated is the leave-all-your-retirement-money-alone part of this step. That you have to do all on your own. And I strongly, seriously, and emphatically encourage you to keep your hands off that money. It's not for you; it's for future you. I know there are times when you may want to draw on these funds to buy a house, pay for college, cover a big medical bill. I get it—these are pricey life events—but do your best to find that money elsewhere. If you ever find yourself considering withdrawing your retirement funds, picture me shaking my clasped hands and begging you, "Don't do it!"

TIFFANY TIP: One way to avoid having to draw on your retirement savings is to not be "house poor." That means you should not pay more than 30% of your budget for housing expenses. If you're above this percentage, consider moving to a less expensive area. Relocating for the sake of a bigger retirement cushion or a fully stocked emergency savings is not a crazy idea but something a super-savvy squirrel would do!

   If you have exhausted all other options and you have to pull some money from your retirement account, investigate the possibility of a loan versus a withdrawal. If and when you pay back a loan, you may be able to avoid early withdrawal penalties or taxes. Also, when you pay back the loan, be sure to double down on your retirement savings efforts to help make up any earnings lost.

DO THE WORK ·······················➤

☐ Set up an automatic transfer into your retirement account.

☐ Give your older self a name, and start saving for her. You are saving to protect her, to house her and keep her healthy. I do it all for my Wanda, whom I honor with my saving-for-retirement efforts! I see you, Wanda, and I save for you.
   My older self's name:

   _____

Investing for Wealth Building

The Plan to Invest for Wealth Building

To improve your quality of living now while leaving a legacy for later, you will need to invest for wealth. Here are the seven steps necessary to get started:

1. Meet the baseline requirements before you start investing.
2. Set investing goals.
3. Determine what type of investor you are.
4. Figure out the best management type for you.
5. Identify the best investment vehicle for you.
6. Start investing.
7. Automate and ignore.

The straightforward goal of investing for wealth is to upgrade your life now, which also means an upgrade in the future. Of course, there's also the secondary goal of achieving a durable type of wealth that may be passed down to your kids or donated to causes that are important to you.

An obvious reason to take additional steps to grow your money is the relentless march of inflation. In the United States, the price of things doubles every twenty years! So, face it: We can't beat inflation, and pretending it doesn't exist certainly doesn't help. But we can use it as an extra incentive to work on building wealth, which is one of the most powerful buffers against inflation.

The good news is that you don't have to have an MBA in finance to start investing. The crash course I'm going to offer you in this section should be enough for you to get going. Pay attention and take notes.

Quick Start: Jump into the Market

Have you ever jumped rope on a playground? I mean when two other people are turning the rope? Most folks rock back and forth trying to find the perfect time to jump in, but the truth is, there's no way to know when that is . . . you just have to *jump*! The same is true for the stock market. Time in the market will beat timing the market any day. The key is to jump in and stay in consistently. In financial terms, this is called dollar-cost averaging (DCA) and means you invest the same dollar amount on a regular basis, regardless of the price of the investment. The advantage of dollar-cost averaging is you'll buy both when prices are low and when they're high. This smooths out your average purchase price. Dollar-cost averaging can be especially powerful in recessions and when the market is down.

For this Quick Start, pick an index fund that mirrors a market, like the S&P 500, and automate an amount of your choosing at least every month. For the last hundred years, the market has generated a yield of around 10%. That means some years were great, some not so great, but the average over time was 10%. So what are you waiting for? Get your dollar-cost averaging on.

Investing for Wealth Building Step 1: Meet the Baseline Requirements Before You Start Investing

As much as I like to say that investing for wealth is a necessity, the reality is that there are other financial matters that take priority. Before you start investing for wealth, you need to have met some criteria. Make sure you can check off every item on the list below before you direct any of your money toward wealth-building investing.

DO THE WORK ·····················➤

☐ I'm on time with my bills. Investing comes with unpredictable risk. Don't sacrifice your current bills for an uncertain outcome.

☐ I am making consistent retirement contributions.

Check this box only if you've started investing for retirement and, if it's available to you, taken advantage of any employer match. Wanda is relying on you to be responsible!

Ideally, you should also have six months of your Noodle Budget saved. In chapter 3, you identified your bare-bones budget, aka Noodle Budget, which covers your basic expenses. Do you have six times this number saved? This would give you an ample cushion to help cover unpredictable life events such as a job loss or significant medical expense. Meet this amount and you may be cleared to begin investing for wealth building.

☐ I have paid off my high-interest-rate debt.

If you're being charged double-digit interest on any debt, you're not likely to outearn what this debt costs you. Pay off your high-interest rate debt before you start trying to earn through investments.

☐ I don't think I'll need the money I invest for the next five years.

While it may not take five years to see a return on stock market investing, it can take close to that amount of time for fluctuations to even out and for you to see any meaningful profit. Check this box if you're ready to say goodbye to your cash long enough to let it grow.

Investing for Wealth Building Step 2: Set Investing Goals

I love goal setting. I think it's a super-helpful way to establish expectations and solidify intention. It also can help you go from daydreaming to planning and commitment.

To help you pin down your investing goals, I have two questions for you. These are simple and straightforward, easy for even you noncommittal types out there to answer!

DO THE WORK ·····················➤

1. How much per month do you want to put into your wealth-building account/s?

    Revisit your budget from page 40 to identify how much you can afford to invest. Remember that covering expenses, saving, paying down high-interest debt, and investing for retirement come first. If you want to be able to invest more, look for areas in your expenses where you may be able to make cuts to carve out more for investing.

2. What's your "why" for wanting to build wealth?

    Are you investing to improve the quality of your life? Or to leave a legacy? Or both? Envision the freedom of choice that extra money could bring to your life, and let this vision help you clarify your purpose with investing.

IRL STORY: CIARA, NEW YORK, NY

I used to believe that you could only invest passively. I would sort of invest a little just to check it off the list, but I didn't put any real thought behind it. I also just generally didn't have a lot of structure to my financial life; I wasn't going through my budget and seeing where I could cut something out or where I might have money left over or identifying specifically what I could allocate toward building wealth or building up my retirement fund.

When I read Tiffany's advice that suggested asking yourself, "What is my why for investing?," that was kind of a pivotal moment for me. It helped me change my strategy. I asked myself, "What are you investing for? What are your goals? Are you investing for wealth building? Are you investing for retirement?" And I realized I wanted to invest for both wealth and retirement. This motivated me to take a detailed look at my budget and see what money I could put into investing.

Eventually, I was able to open a couple of different accounts. I have one brokerage account where my Roth IRA is—I prioritize this since my company doesn't have a 401(k) match—and another that's with a robo-adviser. I also am invested in a couple of ETFs, which are really good if you can't afford an index fund.

Since Tiffany says, "Automate, automate, automate," I have auto-deposits made into each of these accounts. The only one that's not automated is my crypto account, into which I put any "found money." This is just money that a store receipt says I've saved or any kind of rebate check I get.

I know some people are scared of investing because there's so much information. But I was more scared of *not* doing something than I was of doing it. Tiffany helped me understand how to get started, and truthfully, it's totally changed my life—I even transitioned into a career in finance after working in creative services.

Investing for Wealth Building Step 3: Determine What Type of Investor You Are

There are three basic investor types:

1. **Active:** Growth is your focus. You want to build money as quickly as possible, even if it involves a little more risk.
2. **Passive:** Security is your focus. Slow and steady sounds just right. You are willing to earn less if it means you're less likely to lose.
3. **In-Between:** Steady growth is ideal. You're not the biggest risk-taker, but you're willing to take bigger leaps from time to time if it means you'll make more in the long run.

Knowing which one best describes you can help identify which management tool and which investment vehicle will pair well with your personality and preferences. Did you read these descriptions and spot yourself right away? If so, your initial assessment is probably right on . . . but I still suggest you take my quick Identify Your Investor Type quiz below to make sure. There are some questions here that take into account some more practical aspects of investing, such as how much research you're willing to do and how much time you have to spend on this part of your financial life. Don't worry—there are no wrong answers!

DO THE WORK ·····················➤

Read the descriptions below and rate yourself by circling one of the numbers on the scale of 1 to 5, with 1 being least like you and 5 most like you. Be sure to make a selection for Active, Passive, and In-Between.

Research: Do you like reading reviews and/or studying and comparing different versions of products?

Active: *Yes, I love researching my current and potential investments.*

| 1 | 2 | 3 | 4 | 5 |

Passive: *Eh, I'd rather follow tried-and-true trends.*

| 1 | 2 | 3 | 4 | 5 |

In-Between: *A little research can go a long way.*

| 1 | 2 | 3 | 4 | 5 |

Time: How much time do you have to spend managing your wealth-building account?

Active: *I have several hours a week to dedicate to research and management.*

| 1 | 2 | 3 | 4 | 5 |

Passive: *Time? What's that? Let's set it and semiforget it.*

| 1 | 2 | 3 | 4 | 5 |

In-Between: *I have some time to dedicate to research and management but would like to automate some of my investments so I'm in the game even when time is tight.*

| 1 | 2 | 3 | 4 | 5 |

Temperament: Do you have the patience for slow and steady growth? Do you prefer security over excitement?

Active: *Offense! [clap-clap] Offense! [clap-clap] I'm a true planner, and I'm not easily swayed by market movement. Once I have a plan, I trust my plan; I work my plan.*

| 1 | 2 | 3 | 4 | 5 |

Passive: *Um, I'm a little emotional. I get scared and excited easily. Market is up? Me: Yay! I'm rich! Market is down? Me: Oh, no, I'll never recover. Sell! Sell! Sell!*

| 1 | 2 | 3 | 4 | 5 |

In-Between: *I try not to watch every up and down, but huge, long-term swings definitely get my attention, and I might take action as a result.*

| 1 | 2 | 3 | 4 | 5 |

Add up your totals below.

Active: _____

Passive: _____

In-Between: _____

Once you've calculated your scores, look at your totals. Do you have the highest number as an Active, Passive, or In-Between investor? That's your dominant investing personality. Keep it in mind as you work through this section, but know that your investor type isn't set in stone! Use the type you were assigned based on the quiz to help guide you as you get your footing in the land of investing. Once you have your bearings, you may want to make adjustments to your preferences.

Investing for Wealth Building Step 4: Figure Out the Best Management Type for You

When you invest your money with the intention of building wealth, you will need to work with something or someone that manages your funds. This entity might be software through which you make hand-picked stock and other investment selections; a robo-adviser, which is kind of like an algorithm that makes automated investment moves for you; or a financial adviser (the human kind), who will manage your investments with a personal touch. There are pros and cons to each. Let's take a look at them so you can decide what might be the best option for you.

Do-It-Yourself (DIY)

If you want to get your hands directly into the investment mix, there are a couple DIY investor options to consider. You can use an electronic trading platform to buy mutual funds and buy and sell individual stocks and ETFs. Or you can invest through a discount brokerage firm, which will allow you to pick and choose your individual investments, but you'll do so without any guidance from an adviser. Let's look at the pros and cons of these DIY options.

Pros:

- They are low to no cost. DIY options allow you to put all or most of your money directly into investing versus having some of it spent on management/commission fees.
- It can seem fun and exciting to be in control. Just remember that you're playing with real money—*your* real money.

Cons:

- Time and research are essential. This isn't a "con" for everyone, but it's definitely an important consideration when it comes to your time and tolerance for doing the work.
- You won't get any help choosing how to invest based on your risk tolerance. You will have access to resources but no customized guidance.
- There is no automatic rebalancing. Many full-service (and costly) types of investing options will automatically adjust your portfolio if your asset balance falls out of line with your goals.

Robo-Adviser

With a robo-adviser, your investments are managed by a computer or algorithm. This option has higher fees than DIY investing but lower fees than a human financial adviser.

Pros:

- You can get the help you want without paying the higher fees of a financial adviser.

- An intake survey where you indicate your risk tolerance and goals allows for semicustomized investing.
- Automating is super easy; set it, forget it, and let the computer do the work.

Cons:

- You don't have much control over what you invest in.
- There are small fees involved.

Personal Financial Adviser

A financial adviser will provide full-service, fully customized financial planning.

Pros:

- You can get a wide range of finance-based guidance, including on topics such as college planning, debt management, and insurance.
- You get direct attention and can expect next-level customer service.

Cons:

- The management fees can be steep, although they are relative to the amount of assets you have invested. Average fees are around 1% of the total managed assets; if you're quoted or being charged anything above that, negotiate your rate down or shop around.
- There is typically a minimum investment required to work with a financial adviser. The rule of thumb is that you want to have $250,000 of investable assets to make the most of the service and the fees you're being charged.

BUDGETNISTA BREAKDOWN: HOW FINANCIAL ADVISERS ARE PAID

It's important to note that financial advisers are paid differently depending on the type of adviser they may be. There are:

Fee-only financial advisers, who are paid directly by you—the client—for their services.

Fee-based financial advisers, who also get paid by you, the client, but additionally get paid from other sources, like commissions (fees paid as a percentage of the cost of products sold).

Which should you choose? I suggest a fee-only adviser since this type of professional isn't incentivized to sell you products you might not need in order to get their commission. Be sure to check out the money team chapter for how to select a financial adviser if this is the option you think might best suit you.

DO THE WORK ·····················➤

Now that you know the different ways you can invest and how much they might cost, let's decide the direction you want to go in by completing the sentences below.

The best management type for me is _____.

I chose this management type because _____
_____.

The pros of this management type are_____
_____.

The cons of this management type are _____
_____.

The potential cost of this management type is _____.

Investing for Wealth Building Step 5: Identify the Best Investment Vehicle for You

An investment vehicle is whatever you put your money into that you hope will earn a profit. This could be real estate, precious metals, or a business. For our purposes, I want to stay focused on market-based investments, specifically stocks, mutual funds, and ETFs.

We went over some basic definitions of these in the investing for retirement section, but I want to dig a little deeper here to help make sure you are an informed investor. Ready yourself for a quick study session, followed by the satisfaction of being able to say, "Oh yeah, I get it!"

Stocks: A portion of or piece of ownership in a company. Stocks can go up and down in value quickly as they are driven by unpredictable economic factors. They can be bought and sold throughout the trading day, which is from 9:30 a.m. to 4:00 p.m. Eastern Standard Time.

Good for: *Active investors*
Return potential: *High but with high risk*
Fees: *No fees, unless there is one for commissions (which is becoming less and less common)*
Deal maker/breaker: *Can require nerves of steel*

Bonds: An investment in a loan to a company or a state. Bonds are more stable as they are basically a loan that earns interest. That said, with stability comes less opportunity for growth.

Good for: *Passive investors*
Return potential: *Generally secure. Typically provide a moderate, fixed rate of interest.*
Fees: *May include accounting fees, commissions, legal fees, printing costs, registration*

fees, and underwriting fees. Each issuer calculates differently; ask for the breakdown before investing.

Deal maker/breaker: Can help offset the volatility of investing in stocks. But not always a safe bet. If there are interest rate hikes, they can erode the value of bonds.

Mutual Funds: A collection or "basket" of stocks (and/or bonds and other securities) in multiple companies. Unlike stocks, mutual funds cannot be bought and sold throughout the trading day; they can be purchased once daily *after* the stock market closes.

If you buy stocks in a mutual fund, you are buying stocks with a group of other people, which is why it's called a "mutual" fund. You and all the other investors become shareholders of this collective fund.

Good for: Passive investors since greater diversification (a fancy word for more than one company) equals lower risk

Return potential: Medium. All the companies have to go up or down significantly to affect your gain or loss, which means typically neither ups nor downs are going to be major.

Fees: Called an expense ratio (the cost of investing in a mutual fund or exchange-traded fund). Mutual funds tend to have higher fees than ETFs because many are actively managed (by a human).

Deal maker/breaker: Allows for easy auto investing, so you can set it (transfers) and semiforget it. Yay!

Exchange-Traded Funds: An ETF is sort of like the love child of a stock and a mutual fund. It is a group of stocks (and other investments) that is traded on the public exchange during trading hours.

Good for: The in-between investor; someone who wants to walk the line between active and passive investor. If you're intrigued by stocks but intimidated by the risk, this is your baby.

Return potential: *Similar to that of mutual funds. Pretty good, but your gains can only go so high. Less risky than stocks.*

Fees: *Depending on your trading account, there may be fees to buy or sell ETFs called commissions. There are costs to keep the fund running called expense ratios. You should be careful of excessive expense ratios because they can reduce your return/what you make (in most cases, 0.5% will be considered high). The fees are also typically lower than those for a mutual fund.*

Deal breaker/maker: *Auto investing is possible, but the process is not as straightforward as with a mutual fund. You may need to manually go into your account to trade (buy and sell).*

Index Funds: An index fund is also a collection of stocks, but the stocks are invested in a compilation of specific companies that make up an index. These indexes include the S&P 500, the Dow Jones Industrial Average, and the Nasdaq Composite. Index funds are passively managed by a computer and aim to match the market. Computer management means cheaper fees.

Good for: *Passive investors since you're basically telling your money to do whatever the market is doing*

Return potential: *Strong the longer you keep your money invested. Over nearly the last hundred years, the stock market has yielded an average 10% annual return. That means some years have been high, some low, and some in-between. If you leave your money alone, it's more likely to yield that 10% average.*

Fees: *Index funds have fees, but they are typically much lower than those of competing products.*

Deal maker/breaker: *Investing in market indexes requires you to remember that fluctuations are normal. If you're the type to panic and take your money out when the market is temporarily down, index funds may not be for you.*

DO THE WORK ·······················➤

Identify the investment vehicle that speaks most to you and write down why it's the best fit.

Stocks: Fit / Not a fit (circle one)

Why? _____

_____

Mutual Funds: Fit / Not a fit (circle one)

Why? _____

_____

ETFs: Fit / Not a fit (circle one)

Why? _____

_____

Investing for Wealth Building Step 6: Start Investing

So far, this is what you've done:

1. You've determined your investor type. My investor type is:

    ☐ Passive

    ☐ Active

    ☐ In-Between

2. You've chosen your management option. My management option is:

    ☐ DIY brokerage

    ☐ Robo-adviser

    ☐ Financial adviser

3. You've selected your investment vehicle. My investment vehicle is:

☐ Stocks

☐ Mutual funds

☐ ETFs

☐ A little bit of each

By putting all these selections together, you've created your own personal invest-ment profile. Yep, you did it. A sincere "Yay, you!" is warranted for all the work you did to get this far.

If you're feeling like the vision is still a bit fuzzy, let's take a look at how these three factors might combine to create a real-life investor. Meet my friends Amanda, Pauline, Parker, Maureen, and Benin.

Active Amanda's Investment Profile

(Active; DIY brokerage; stocks)

Amanda has a DIY brokerage account linked to her checking account and spends a few hours a week researching stocks, trading, and managing her investment portfolio.

Pro: Her wealth can grow fast.

Con: The risk of losing money is high.

Passive Pauline's Investment Profile

(Passive; robo-adviser; mutual fund)

Pauline is not sure where to start, so she opens an account with a robo-adviser. She takes robo's investment survey, and an algorithm automatically chooses her invest-ments based on the risk tolerance and goals revealed by the survey. She automatically contributes to her robo-adviser account each month.

Pro: Steady growth leads to legacy creation. Her account is passively managed, so fees are low.

Con: To see a decent return, she will have to leave her money alone for at least five years.

Passive Parker's Investment Profile

(Passive; financial planner; ETFs and stocks)

Parker has a super-successful business and makes six figures a year. He wants help with his full financial future but is not sure where to start and doesn't have much time. Parker hires a financial planner. His planner invests his money in a mix of ETFs and stocks.

Pro: He gets step-by-step guidance on more than just his investments (e.g., insurance, debt management, taxes, estate planning).

Con: He chooses a fee-based versus a fee-only financial planner, who is earning a 1.5% on his assets under management (AUM) and commissions (fees paid as a percentage of the cost of products sold) from financial products that she purchases from them (e.g., insurance). The cost of this level of service will significantly minimize his return in the long run.

In-Between Maureen's Investment Profile

(In-between; DIY brokerage; ETFs)

Maureen enjoys trading ETFs via a DIY brokerage firm, which lets her get a taste of stocks but gives her a little more safety since ETFs are a group of stocks (and other investments); that is, she doesn't have all her eggs in one basket.

Pro: She pays low fees and has medium control.

Con: Her money is doing the work but not necessarily getting big returns.

In-Between Benin's Investment Profile

(In-between; discount brokerage; mutual fund)

Benin doesn't have much time and doesn't feel confident in his ability to invest, so he chooses an actively managed (but not by him) mutual fund and hopes to beat the market over time.

Pro: With his excess money invested rather than sitting in a savings account, growth will likely be slow but steady.

Con: He is likely *not* going to be rolling in dough during his peak years. He is paying higher fees (expense ratio) for the convenience of a managed fund, but it's not likely that the mutual fund will outperform a passively managed ETF. Just 20% of active U.S. stock fund managers beat their benchmark after fees in 2022.

DO THE WORK ·····················➤

If you've determined you're an active investor:
- ☐ Open a DIY or discount brokerage account.
- ☐ Research stocks.
- ☐ Purchase stocks.

If you've determined you're a passive investor:
- ☐ Consider hiring a financial adviser or research a mutual fund that fits your financial goals.
- ☐ Set up automatic transfers.
- ☐ Keep an eye on the fees.

If you're an in-between/ETF investor:
- ☐ Open a DIY or discount brokerage account.
- ☐ Choose an index fund that mirrors a specific index like the S&P 500.

If you're not sure where to start and you have $250,000 or more to invest:
- ☐ Research financial advisers, ideally certified financial planners, who can help you manage your assets—more on this type of finance pro in the money team chapter.

Investing for Wealth Building Step 7: Automate and Ignore

All that remains for you to do is to make sure you've got your investment system set up to succeed. This means automating when possible and letting your money grow undisturbed over time.

The key to not disturbing your money is to ignore the noise—that is, news—that comes out of the investing world. If you've never tuned in, I suggest keeping it that way. (The one exception to this rule is if you are invested in only one stock; in this case, you want to keep an eye on any major company changes that may suggest it's time to move your money.) Because once you start tuning in, you'll realize the stock squawking never stops. And ultimately, the day-to-day ups and downs of the market should do little to influence how you invest.

Remember, when you invest, you've got to be ready to play the long game. This is why, as you may remember, I wanted to make sure you felt comfortable without your investing funds for at least five years.

DO THE WORK ·······························➤

Check these boxes once the tasks have been completed:

- [ ] I've set up recurring deposits to my investing account *or* set an alarm on my calendar that reminds me when to trade.
- [ ] I'm a calm, cool investor; I'm not using market news to influence how I invest.
- [ ] If appropriate, I'm staying on top of news about the one company I'm invested in.

The Invest Like an Insider Review

You've learned how to automate investments into retirement and brokerage accounts and increase contributions as income increases.

60% FINANCIALLY WHOLE

This is a big deal. You've put yourself on course to achieving 100% financial peace of mind.

CHAPTER 8

70% Whole
Get Good with Insurance

If I walked into a party and said, "All right, who wants to talk insurance with me?!," I'd probably spend the rest of the night talking to myself. This is because insurance isn't exactly exciting, and no one wants to spend that much time thinking about it, let alone discussing it. Yet it is one of the best tools for managing risk, and it's an essential component of financial wholeness. The reason you get insurance is to protect yourself and your assets in case something happens, and in this unpredictable thing called life, *things happen*. You want to be ready when they do.

If you are thinking of skipping or skimming this chapter because you're already covered . . . please don't. You might be surprised to discover what it really means to have good coverage. I always thought I was all set with insurance until I met with my financial adviser, Anjali, who said, "Tiffany, although you look like you're in your twenties, your insurance does too." OK, maybe she didn't say that at forty, I looked like I was in my twenties, but she *did* say that I had the insurance of a twenty-something, and was severely underinsured.

Now let's get to the types of insurance you want to consider, along with the different types of coverage and how to determine what's best for you based on your age or stage of life.

The Plan to Get Good with Insurance

Let's make sure you have proper insurance coverage in the areas of health, life, disability, and property and casualty (e.g., home and auto). To do this, you'll work through four steps:

1. Get health insurance.
2. Explore life insurance.
3. Explore disability insurance.
4. Get property and casualty insurance.

WHAT YOU'LL NEED

✓ Any policy details on coverage you've secured for yourself in the areas of health, life, disability, and/or home and auto insurance
✓ Any policy details on coverage obtained through an employer or other party

> ### Quick Start
>
> If you want to get a head start on getting good with insurance, visit one of the insurance sites I like (see the *Made Whole* tool kit at madewholeworkbook.com for the most up-to-date list) to perform a checkup on your coverage. If the site suggests that you're deficient in a specific type of insurance, focus on getting that coverage up to speed this week.

Get Good with Insurance Step 1: Get Health Insurance

Health insurance is an agreement between you and an insurance company that covers your health-related costs in exchange for consistent payment to them of what's called an annual premium that most people pay monthly. Regardless of how old or young you are, it's always smart to have some coverage.

How It Works: If you work for an employer, you will typically be offered options for healthcare coverage and get to select what type of plan will work best for you. If you are self-employed or seeking independent coverage, you can often access the same plans, but they come at a higher cost.

There are a few types of plans, including HMO, PPO, and high deductible with an HSA (I'll give you a detailed look at each of these shortly). These plans vary primarily based on three factors:

1. **Deductible:** The amount you pay for healthcare costs before your insurance plan kicks in.
2. **Coinsurance:** The percentage of a total bill that you'll be responsible for paying after you've met your deductible.
3. **Out-of-pocket max:** The most you'll pay out of pocket; once you hit this cap, your insurance pays 100% of the costs.

How your premium cost is determined: The premium is the amount you will pay each month for your coverage regardless of how much or how little you use your insurance. Your health insurance premium varies based on plan type, your age, the state in which you live, and how many people are covered under the policy.

Health Insurance Homework

When the time comes for you to select health insurance, you will be presented with a *lot* of information, which will likely include acronyms and plenty of language that seems foreign (unless you work in insurance). You can take some of the confusion away by reviewing this section beforehand.

Types of Plans

HDHPs: High-deductible health plans have a higher deductible but offer the benefit of letting you contribute to a health savings account, or HSA. These types of plans work great for young and healthy people who have minimal medical expenses during the year. In most cases, HDHPs cover preventive services, such as immunizations, screening tests, and checkups, so you can stay healthy (even if you can't stay young!).

Note: High-deductible plans typically have lower monthly premiums than other types of plans.

PPOs: Preferred provider organization plans allow you to see any provider as long as they are in a specific network. A network is a group of doctors, specialists, or healthcare centers like a hospital that have agreed to take insurance from a particular company. A PPO plan might be right for you if you have an illness, preexisting conditions, daredevil little kids, or any other known factor that may lead to high medical expenses and/or the need for specialists.

Note: A PPO will generally have higher monthly premium payments and a lower deductible. This type of plan does not offer an HSA (health savings account), but some employers may provide access to an FSA (flexible spending account).

HMOs: Health maintenance organization plans are usually the most affordable of the plans offered. This is because under an HMO plan, your primary care doctor will manage all your healthcare services, keep track of all your medical records, and provide routine care. This primary doctor will also provide you with referrals to specialists as needed.

Note: HMO plans don't offer you the flexibility of a PPO; you will have to see a physician within the HMO network (if you want the maximum coverage that the plan provides). You also won't have access to an HSA, but you may be able to fund an FSA.

Additional Options: Healthcare Expense Accounts

If you receive healthcare benefits from your employer, you've likely fought your way through the open enrollment process and somewhere in your review maybe noticed a mention of FSA and HSA accounts. These are accounts that allow you to save tax-free money that can be used to pay for qualifying medical expenses. Understanding the difference between the two can help you make a decision about what insurance coverage type is best for you.

A FLEXIBLE SPENDING ACCOUNT (FSA):

- Is available to you if offered by your employer; typically, there's no requirement to be enrolled in any type of health plan to gain access
- Allows you to save pretax money for qualified, out-of-pocket medical expenses, such as copays, prescriptions, and dental- and vision-related costs
- Allows tax-free withdrawals (also called distributions) to pay for qualifying out-of-pocket medical expenses
- Allows automated payroll contributions, if accessed through your employer
- Is a use-it-or-lose-it plan, meaning that any pre-tax contribution you make must be used by the end of the year or it's forfeited

A HEALTH SAVINGS ACCOUNT (HSA):

- Is available to you only if you have a high-deductible health plan (see page 170)
- Lets you save pretax money for qualified out-of-pocket medical expenses like doctor visits, copays, dental and vision costs, and prescriptions
- Allows tax-free withdrawals (also called distributions), as long as the money is used for qualified out-of-pocket medical expenses
- Allows automated payroll contributions, if accessed through your employer
- Can accept contributions from employers and even some insurers. If your insurance company makes a contribution, it's done through something called a

"premium pass through contribution," which means that part of the premium you pay gets automatically transferred to your HSA.

- Does not expire at the end of a calendar year, and you can take the money with you if you leave your job
- Presents an amazing opportunity for a retirement hack (see sidebar)

HSA RETIREMENT HACK

Looking for an outside-the-box way to grow your retirement funds? Consider an HSA, which lets you transfer the funds you've set aside for medical expenses to a qualified brokerage account (while keeping it available to you if needed). Once in the brokerage account, your money can earn interest just like it would in a 401(k) or IRA.

An HSA is also triple tax advantaged: Your contributions go in pretax, they grow tax free, and they come out tax free. Further, you can assign a beneficiary (the person who gets the money when you pass) to the HSA, so if you don't use the funds, they go to your designated beneficiary. Seriously, there are so many reasons to love this hack.

To take advantage of it, you'll need to have a high-deductible health plan (keep in mind that HDHPs aren't right for everyone) and then work with the HSA custodian to help you get your account linked to a brokerage firm.

Insurance and Special Circumstances

Your health insurance needs don't lessen when you're unemployed or retired; in fact, they may increase, especially during retirement. Here are some resources to explore depending on your circumstances.

If you are unemployed: Visit the Health Insurance Marketplace at HealthCare .gov to determine what health coverage you are eligible for. If you meet the income and resource limits and are age sixty-five or older, or are under age sixty-five and blind or disabled, you could also qualify for free or low-cost coverage through Medicaid. If you're under nineteen, also check to see if you qualify for the Children's Health Insurance Program (CHIP).

If you are retired: Your options vary based on your age. If you retire "early," which is any time before sixty-five, you can apply for insurance through the Health Care Marketplace. You can apply at any point and don't have to wait for an open enrollment period.

If you are sixty-five or older, you are eligible for Medicare. Medicare has two parts: Part A (hospital insurance) and Part B (medical insurance). If you or your spouse worked and paid Medicare taxes for at least ten years, you are eligible for premium-free Part A. Part B comes with a fee for everyone, regardless of taxes paid.

DO THE WORK ·······························➤

You'd be surprised how often people don't know what type of coverage they have or what it includes. While health insurance has gotten more expensive, it's also gotten more expansive. You might have access to prescription benefits, infertility programs, and child-care and/or elder-care assistance. Make sure you're taking advantage of everything available to you.

My health insurance plan:

Name: _____

Type of insurance: _____

FSA or HSA: _____

Deductible: _____

Notes:

Could be better: _____

Is your deductible too high? Is there a doctor you want/need to see who's out of network?

*Benefits I've been missing out on:*_____

    Does your plan offer reimbursement for certain supplements or medications, or provide wellness benefits that you're not using?

Get Good with Insurance Step 2: Explore Life Insurance

Like health insurance, life insurance is a contract between the policyholder (you) and the insurer (insurance company). You pay a premium to the insurer and you receive coverage. The coverage in this case is known as a death benefit because it pays out to your beneficiaries only upon your passing. Yep, you are literally buying insurance on your life.

A lot of people tend to shy away from life insurance because it's an undeniable confrontation with their own mortality. But the reality is, it doesn't protect you—it protects those you provide for financially, and that's whom you want to think of as you explore life insurance. If your income supports others (immediate family, extended family, or others), a life insurance policy can allow you to continue to care for your loved ones even when you are gone.

A key factor in life insurance is timing. Since you have to pay a premium, you don't want to get it earlier than is necessary. However, it's generally less expensive when you are younger and less likely to have health issues, so you don't want to wait too long. If you have children, other dependents, or any sizable debts, it should be a priority regardless of your age.

If this all sounds confusing, don't worry—I've provided a checklist at the end of this section to help you determine your customized coverage needs. Before we get to that, let me give you some more background on how life insurance works and what types you might come across when you start shopping for it.

How Life Insurance Works

When you apply for life insurance, you provide personal health information in exchange for a quote of what it might cost to cover you. The information you'll be required to submit will include basic stuff, such as your gender, age, and weight, along with some more specific details pertaining to your medical history. For example, they will likely want to know if you are a current or former smoker or if you have any preexisting health conditions.

It's smart to gather quotes from a few different companies or at least based on different death benefit amounts. Once you have these in hand, you can select the one that seems best for you and start the more extensive application process. This process can include completing more forms and, in some cases, taking what is basically a physical. You'll likely get your glucose levels, blood pressure, cholesterol, and so on checked.

The life insurance company will then analyze all your information and issue a formal offer with the cost of your monthly premium and how much the policy will offer on your passing. By the way, you're not locked into anything whatsoever at this point—you've simply received what's considered a more fully vetted estimate. Don't sign anything until you've reviewed all the policy terms.

How the Cost of Insurance Is Determined

The cost of life insurance is determined by how long an insurer thinks you're going to live (based on all the information they've gathered about you) before they would have to pay out on your death benefit. To a life insurance company, you are merely a collection of numbers that translates to a risk-return ratio, and they use this to calculate your premium cost. This is why, as I mentioned earlier, there's a cost benefit to you if you secure life insurance when you are younger and healthier. Less risk equals lower cost.

I know it all seems kind of morbid to think of a company essentially gambling on your life, but for them it's not personal. And I actually think we can take a cue from life insurance companies here—we too can set aside the personal or emotional nature of the decision and instead focus on the protection being offered.

IRL STORY: TIFFANY, NEWARK, NJ

My beloved husband, Jerrell Smith, was a superstrong and fit person—it was part of why I called him Superman. Yet he had his kryptonite, which was a predisposition to aneurysms. He had his first diagnosed aneurysm when he was thirty-four years old. As you can imagine, a life insurance company might not be too eager to cover someone who's had a near-fatal aneurysm, or the coverage would have been astronomically high. But thankfully, Jerrell had already gotten life insurance four years prior when his daughter (my stepdaughter), Alyssa, was five.

When he passed away suddenly at age forty-one from a second aneurysm in 2021, the payout on this policy allowed the hopes and dreams he had for Alyssa to live on. When the time comes, she will have the money to pay for college or put toward buying a home.

Types of Life Insurance Plans

There are two types of life insurance plans: term life insurance and permanent life insurance (this includes universal and whole). Let's dive a little deeper into each.

Term life insurance: As the name suggests, this type of plan covers you for a specific term, which is usually a set number of years. For example, you might get a thirty-year policy, and this is how long your coverage would last. During the thirty years, you would pay your monthly premium, and if you were to pass away, your beneficiaries would receive the payout. If you were to still be alive, God willing, after thirty years, your policy would expire, and the death benefit would no longer exist.

Some people avoid getting term life insurance because they feel frustrated by the thought of paying for something that never pays out. Yet if it doesn't pay out, it means you're still among the living, which I think most people would consider preferable to a payout. I can see how it's a tricky bit of logic to sort out, but my advice is to think about it like you might any other type of insurance—do you pay for car, home, health, or pet insurance and get upset when you don't have to file a claim due to an accident or injury or loss? Are you sad that your dog didn't get sick and have to use the insurance you paid for? My guess is probably not.

You can find a life insurance carrier that will offer you an option to convert a term policy to a permanent policy at the end of the term. This conversion is usually quite costly, but it's out there if you want to explore the option.

Note: Term life insurance is suitable for probably 99% of the population. If you get it when you're relatively young and healthy, it's usually not too expensive. Plus, you can usually get a term that covers most of your working years, which is when the coverage would mean the most.

As an example, let's say you are thirty-five years old and you get a thirty-year policy. This would mean a death benefit would be paid out until you were age sixty-five, the standard retirement age. If you were to pass away anytime between thirty-five and sixty-five, your beneficiaries would receive the money from your life insurance policy during the years you would have otherwise provided for them financially (this is in the instance of beneficiaries who are your dependents or a spouse or relative you support).

Permanent life insurance (also referred to as whole life or universal): This type of plan covers you until your death, regardless of when that occurs. This is why it's referred to as "permanent" or "whole life." With permanent life insurance, you pay a monthly premium, and a portion of what you pay also accumulates a cash value that you can access at a certain point. On the surface, this seems like a much sweeter deal than what a term policy might offer you, but a closer look reveals some not-so-sweet details:

- **If an insurance broker is trying to sell you on this product, they have a conflict of interest**—insurance brokers make *a lot* more money when they sell a permanent policy versus a term one. So if they're pushing a permanent policy, you want to make sure to consider whom that sale is going to benefit more: you or them?

- **The cash value is unlikely to be more than what you'd earn through investing**—your out-of-pocket premium payments for permanent life insurance will be significantly higher than what you will pay for term insurance. While a portion of your payments toward a permanent policy will build a cash value, the earnings do not even come close to what the difference in cost could potentially make if it were invested in the stock market. Let me put this in numbers so you can see clearly what I mean.

  For a $1,000,000 death benefit, a healthy, nonsmoking thirty-year-old woman could pay as little as $40 per month for thirty years for a term policy, or $730 per month for a permanent policy. (Yes, it's that much more!)

  For one year, your out-of-pocket cost comparison would look like this: $480 (term) versus $8,760 (permanent), a difference of $8,280 (for just *one year*). If you were instead to take that money ($8,280) and invest it in the stock market, it could yield a return of 10% (that's $828); 10% is the average yield the market has produced for nearly the last hundred years.

  Conversely, for every $100 you invest in whole life insurance, the first $5 goes to purchase the insurance itself. That's it! If we use our $730 example above, a little over $35 is actually going toward the coverage part of your policy. The other $695 goes to the cash value buildup from your investment. Here's the crazy part: For about the first three years, your money goes to fees alone.

  Chiiiile, it doesn't get much better after the first three years, either. The average rate of return after those three years of making nada, zilch, zero will be about 1.2% on that $8,340 ($695 × 12). If that money were to sit in your permanent life insurance policy, it might average a rate of return around 1.2%, or around $100. Depending on when you're reading this book, a high-yield savings account could provide a much better return than this "investment."

  To add insult to injury, do you know who gets the cash value of your policy if you pass away without spending it? If you guessed your beneficiaries, you're wrong. When you pass away, cash value typically reverts to the life insurance company. Your beneficiaries receive the policy's death benefit amount, minus any loans and withdrawals of cash value you made.

Now, these aren't precise numbers since they're based on average annual rates of return, but they're ballpark figures that make my point: There are better ways to build your wealth than a permanent life insurance policy.

- **Nearly half of permanent life insurance policyholders stop making payments within the first ten years and never see a return**—you usually have to make it to around ten years of payments on a permanent policy to see any real cash value build (1.2% doesn't grow that fast!). But, according to the Society of Actuaries, 45% of whole life insurance policyholders surrender their policies within the first ten years. This means that you lose out on any perceived cash value benefits of this type of policy, and you also face potentially higher costs for term insurance (since you'll be older when you make the switch).

  Note: There are people for whom a permanent policy makes sense, and those people are basically the 1%. These are people who have maxed out every single pretax, tax-deferred bucket available to them and still have so much excess savings that they just need another place to stash some cash and let it earn a little baby bit of interest. If you fit this description, I would suggest that you ask your certified financial planner (CFP)—if you trust them and they won't set you up to be featured on some scandalous *Dateline* story—if permanent life insurance is something you should explore. Don't start by asking someone who sells life insurance—you know what they're likely to say!

At the end of the day, I consider life insurance a tool for protection, not for earning money, so the appeal of a permanent policy isn't there—especially considering the excessive expense and the better investment options. I advise against it for my family and friends, and I pass the same advice along to you.

DO THE WORK ·······················➤

Let's figure out if you need life insurance, and if so, how much and what type.

Do I Need Life Insurance?

Your need for life insurance will depend primarily upon whether you financially support others and if you have any significant debts. Circle yes or no below to see where you stand.

1. I own property Y/N
2. I have dependents Y/N
3. I am the primary wage earner and support my family, extended family, or others Y/N
4. I have debt (car loan, mortgage, private student loans, credit card debt, etc.) Y/N

Any yes would put you in the position of potentially needing life insurance. If you circled yes for question 3, you need life insurance yesterday.

How Much Life Insurance Do I Need?

Your needs will vary based on a few factors: your income, the size of your household, your monthly expenses, your debt, and future goals that you want to ensure are funded. You can get a sense of the starting amount for your policy by using a general rule of thumb, which is to insure yourself for a minimum of ten times your income, and ideally fifteen times.

If you make more than $300,000, this calculation might get you more insurance than you need or cost too much to justify the amount of coverage. In this case, you would be better off aiming to insure the cost of twenty years of your expenses.

Calculate Your Needs—Income of Under $300,000 Per Year

Multiply your income by at least 10 and ideally by 15.

Example:

$80,000 annual income × 10 = $800,000 insurance policy

$80,000 annual income × 15 = $1.2 million insurance policy

_____ *[insert your annual income] × 10 =* _____

_____ *[insert your annual income] × 15 =* _____

Calculate Your Needs—Income of $300,000 or More Per Year

Multiply the total of your monthly expenses by 12 to get your annual expense total, then multiply this figure by 20.

Example:

$10,000 monthly expenses × 12 = $120,000 × 20 = $2.5 million insurance policy

_____ *[insert your monthly expenses] × 12 =* _____ *× 20 =* _____

What Type of Life Insurance Should I Get?

Based on the descriptions I offered earlier, circle which type of insurance you think *I think* would be best for you:

Term

Term

OK, OK . . . it's possible I did that on purpose. I've probably made it clear enough that I believe term insurance is likely the best option for most people; as in, you are "most people."

How Long Should My Policy Be For?

The goal of life insurance is to protect your working years since ideally you will have other assets to take care of your family after you retire. So really the length of your policy will depend on how long you plan on working, but generally you can think of wanting it to get you to the age of sixty-five. That would mean getting a thirty-year policy if you're under thirty-five, a twenty-year policy if you're under forty-five, and a ten-year policy if you're fifty-five or older.

I generally don't recommend getting insurance to also cover you during retirement, since again the primary purpose of a policy is to cover your working years. If you have a disabled child who will never be fully self-sufficient or adult children who will continue to be financially dependent, it could make sense to consider a permanent policy if it's a cost that won't be too great of a burden to you.

> **TIFFANY TIP:** For many families, life insurance can be a way to leave behind wealth not accessible during your life. It's possible to leave your beneficiaries millions of dollars even if you weren't a millionaire when you were alive. At the very least, you want to ensure that there's enough insurance money to cover your funeral expenses and any major debt you might leave behind.

How to Shop for and Secure Life Insurance

If you're ready to shop for life insurance, I keep an updated list of reputable companies in the online tool kit. You can also request a quote through a company you already trust, but note that there are no "bundle" discounts offered with life and other types of insurance.

In most cases, you can generate a cost quote and complete most of your initial life insurance shopping online. However, if you have any kind of preexisting medical condition, you should consider using an agent to help you seek out the best options. An agent will be able to do some research based on your condition and narrow down the list of companies that may have the best policy for you. Keep in mind that the agent will receive a commission from the insurance policy you choose.

Life Insurances Quotes and Notes

Use this space to document any companies you've contacted or any that are definitely not on your list. Questions? Quotes? Make note of them here.

_____

_____

_____

_____

_____

IRL STORY: TAMIKA, HAMLET, NC

A few years ago, I thought I was doing OK with my insurance. I had auto, home, and even life and disability through my employer. As a single parent and the breadwinner, I was focused on the money side of things—as in, let me try to make more money and invest more to take care of everyone.

But Tiffany's advice made me realize I had to look at how much insurance I had and if it was enough for my family. I had to say to myself, *Hey, Tamika, you have two boys. If you do leave from here, will the life that you want for them be achievable with what you have set up?* And the answer to that question was no. Not even with just the life insurance piece, but even if something happened to my job or my car, or if I had a really big accident or something seriously damaged my home . . . I wasn't covered in the way I needed to be.

Some of the changes I made included increasing the liability limit on my auto insurance so that it was higher than my state's minimum requirement, which just wasn't enough. I also got insurance to cover my jewelry. I have a homeowner's policy, but it wouldn't have covered the value of those items. So I added jewelry insurance, and it's only $5 a month.

In the area of life insurance, I increased it to cover ten to fifteen years of my annual income. I also got additional life insurance outside of my current employer. It was really scary to me to realize that if I left my job, I wouldn't have a policy to protect my kids. And that if I didn't have that coverage, the financial burden could fall on my family members. I didn't want that, and I didn't want my family to have to start a GoFundMe or sell food in order to raise money for a funeral (as is customary in my family). I wanted to have the peace of knowing everything would be covered.

I also got separate disability insurance and a long-term care policy. I'm only forty-seven, but a rare disease runs in my family, and I knew just from life experiences that I needed better coverage. I knew I didn't want to make the same mistakes I've seen other people in my family make. I've seen firsthand the financial effects of everyone trying to help because insurance typically only covers so much. I've seen the younger generation have to pull from their future to take care of their parents—and I don't want my children to be burdened with that. Tiffany really helped open my eyes more to all this and get ahead of anything that could happen.

Get Good with Insurance Step 3: Explore Disability Insurance

Disability insurance is a financial product designed to cover you if you lose the ability to collect your paycheck due to illness or injury. It's an important type of insurance that frankly gets overlooked too often.

How It Works

Disability insurance will cover a percentage of your income should something happen to you that leaves you unable to work, either short- or long-term. A lot of people assume that if they had a need for disability coverage, they could rely on what's offered through their employer, state disability benefits, or a combination of the two to get them through. But sometimes these options, even when combined, can leave you short either because it's not enough money or because your specific injury or illness prevents you from receiving 100% of the benefits. Whatever the case, you don't want to find out that it's not enough after you need it.

How the Cost Is Determined

The cost of disability insurance is based on a handful of factors, including:

- **Your age:** Generally, the younger you are, the lower the cost.
- **Your gender:** Women tend to file more disability claims, including those related to pregnancy and childbirth, so their disability insurance is typically more expensive. When shopping for a policy, look for a provider that offers a "unisex" rate.
- **Your overall health:** Similar to life insurance, disability insurance can require a medical checkup.
- **Your occupation:** Generally, the higher the risk of your work or your lifestyle, the higher the cost. If you work in a job where your risk of injury is high, disability insurance will necessarily be more expensive for you.
- **Your income:** Higher income means a higher potential payout for the insurer, which will increase your premium.
- **Whether or not you smoke:** If you are a smoker, you will pay more.
- **The length of the benefit period:** The greater the length of coverage, the higher the cost of your premium.
- **How disability is defined by the policy:** Disability insurance that covers your inability to work your specific job (called own-occupation) is less expensive than a policy that covers your ability to work in any job (called any-occupation).

Types of Disability Insurance

We're going to focus on short- and long-term disability insurance as these are the most common types.

Short-term disability insurance (STDI) is often offered through your employer and will usually cover between three and six months (although it can cover up to a year) of lost income due to illness, injury, or parental leave. It can provide up to 80% of your income.

Note: While private STDI is available, it can be more expensive than it's worth, and you might be better off putting the money you'd pay toward a premium into an emergency savings fund.

Long-term disability insurance (LTDI) offers coverage that can last years, and policies typically will provide 40 to 60% of your income for the length of the term. The term, however, doesn't usually kick in right away. The idea here is that a short-term disability policy will have been covering you from the moment you started needing it through several months (depending on the length of the term on your STDI).

Note: Since LTDI has a waiting period that happens before you collect benefits, people often have to rely on STDI or emergency savings to bridge the income gap until this long-term coverage kicks in.

Determining Your Disability Insurance Needs

Let's identify your specific needs for disability insurance. Since it typically doesn't make sense to get a STDI policy through a private insurance company, I'm going to focus the discussion here on what type of long-term policy could be best for you.

Do I Need Disability Insurance?

Here's a quick checklist to see if you need long-term disability coverage. Check all that apply.

☐ I am earning income.

☐ I am accumulating wealth (that I want to protect!).

☐ I have people who are financially dependent on me.

☐ I am self-employed.

If you checked any of the above items, I encourage you to consider getting long-term disability insurance.

How Much Disability Insurance Do I Need?

As I mentioned, long-term disability can cover anywhere from 40 to 60% of your income. Obviously, the more you can collect, the better, so you'll want to get 60% of your income covered if possible. The premium amount does go up as the percentage of coverage does, so you will need to make sure it makes financial sense for you to pay a higher premium.

Aim for: A plan that would cover 60% of your income

What Should the Duration of My Policy Be?

You're going to pay more for longer versus shorter coverage. In an ideal scenario, you will have coverage that will last you until retirement, but depending on how old you are, it may be too costly to get coverage for that long.

Aim for: A policy that lasts until retirement

What Should I Look for in a Long-Term Disability Policy?

Any-occupation coverage will not cover you if you can still work in some capacity. In other words, the expectation is that you may still be able to work at a job that's different from your own.

Own-occupation coverage will cover you even if you can work in a job different from your own.

If you are a specialist in any field, it's important to focus on an own-occupation policy. This is especially true if you put a lot of time, effort, and/or money into training and education for your current job.

For example, if you're a doctor, you definitely want an own-insurance policy because you likely spent many years and a lot of money to be able to do your job. If something were to happen to you and you had an any-occupation policy, you might not receive all of your claim since depending on your injury or illness, you could be considered potentially capable of working in another capacity.

Aim for: An own-occupation policy, especially if you are in a specialized career

DO THE WORK ·····················➤

There are details you will want to know about long-term disability insurance. If you are employed by a company, check in with your HR department and request the information that would help you fill in the blanks below. If your company does not offer any LTDI coverage or if you are self-employed, use these as prompts to help you shop for and compare policies.

- My out-of-pocket premium costs are:

_____

_____

_____

- The percentage of my income that would be covered if I filed a claim is:

_____

_____

_____

- The kind of event or injury that would trigger a payout is:

_____

_____

_____

- The length of time my disability would pay out for is:

_____

_____

_____

- The amount of time I would have to wait until I received my first payment* is:

_____

_____

_____

---

* This is super important! If you discover that it would take months to receive your first payment, you want to make certain that you have funds that could get you to that point. These funds could come from STDI or your emergency savings or a combination of the two.

Get Good with Insurance Step 4: Get Property and Casualty Insurance

You probably have some form of property and casualty insurance yet don't know it by that name. Also known as P&C insurance, this is the coverage you would get on your home, auto, or motorcycle, and on any type of recreational vehicle such as a boat or an RV.

In this context, "property" refers to any kind of tangible, physical item you want to insure. And "casualty" describes coverage of your liability should you be found legally responsible for an accident that causes injuries to another person.

We're going to focus on auto and home insurance since these are the most widely needed forms of P&C insurance. You likely need coverage if you drive a vehicle or if you own or rent a home. Even if you already have coverage, I encourage you to keep reading to find out if you have enough coverage (most people don't!).

Auto Insurance

If you have a car, you'd better have insurance on it. Not only because it's required by almost every state in the United States, but because if you are found to be at fault in any accident, you will be financially responsible for the cost of repairs and/or replacement. And trust me—you don't want to be on the hook for any kind of car repairs; even just a buff out of a bumper can cost you as much as a month's worth of groceries. If you get into an accident while driving someone else's car, as long as you had permission to drive their vehicle, their insurance should cover the accident. If the total damages exceed their policy limits, you would then file a claim with your own insurance company for the remaining costs.

How It Works

You pay a monthly premium to an auto insurance provider in exchange for coverage should you be involved in an accident.

How the Cost Is Determined

There are several factors that determine the cost of your auto coverage, including:

- Your driving record
- Your vehicle
- Where you live
- How your car is stored (e.g., in a garage or on the street)
- How far you drive on a regular basis
- The amount of your deductible—as with health insurance, a higher deductible will cost you less up front but more should you need to use your insurance

Types of Auto Insurance

Auto coverage varies based on the different risks related to owning and operating a vehicle. Here are the main types of coverage and what exactly they cover:

- Collision = damages to your car
- Comprehensive = theft, vandalism, weather events, accidents with animals
- Personal injury protection (PIP) = medical expenses and loss of wages related to bodily injury resulting from an accident
- Uninsured/underinsured motorists = for when the other driver doesn't have insurance or enough coverage to fix your car
- Liability = injuries and property damage if you're at fault in an accident

DO THE WORK ·····················➤

The key with auto insurance is to make sure you have enough coverage. Being in an accident is stressful enough; you don't want to add excessive unexpected expenses to the list of your concerns. Use this itemized list to see if your current policy has you properly covered or to help you get everything you need in a new policy.

1. **Household drivers:** Everyone who will be driving the car should be covered.
☐ All good
☐ Needs updating

Note: _____

2. **Vehicle information:** Check the year, make, and model of the car or cars listed on your policy to be sure they match what you're driving these days.
☐ All good
☐ Needs updating

Note: _____

3. **Bodily injury:** This covers another driver's or passenger's injuries in a car accident where you are at fault. The minimum amount of coverage required varies by state, but the most common liability limits related to bodily injury are $25,000 in bodily injury per person and $50,000 in total bodily injury per accident. That sounds like a lot, but medical care can be expensive, so be sure to look into the costs of carrying more than your state's minimum requirement. According to insurance giant Progressive's website, you want your total bodily injury per accident to exceed your net worth (you'll learn how to calculate this in chapter 9), which essentially represents what you have to lose if someone were to sue you for damages. For example, if your net worth is $90,000, then a good car insurance policy for you would offer $100,000 in total bodily injury coverage per accident.
☐ All good
☐ Needs updating

Note: _____
☐ Don't need

4. **Property damage:** This helps pay for damage to someone else's property because of an accident you caused. This coverage should, like that for bodily injury,

meet or exceed your net worth. If that's cost prohibitive for you, obtain a policy that offers you the most coverage at a cost that's within your budget.

☐ All good

☐ Needs updating

Note: _____

5. **Medical coverage:** This may help pay your or your passengers' medical expenses if you're injured in a car accident, regardless of who caused the accident. If you have health insurance, medical coverage can also help cover your out-of-pocket costs, such as your deductible. Medical coverage may be offered through something known as Med-Pay, which is an additional coverage option for auto insurance policies in most states. Some states offer what's called personal injury protection instead of Med-Pay.

While you're typically not legally required to carry medical coverage, it's a good idea if you can afford it. Good coverage would be that which offers a higher limit than your health insurance deductible. This way, Med-Pay or PIP could cover your deductible along with other related medical costs.

☐ All good

☐ Needs updating

Note: _____

6. **Uninsured motorist bodily injury:** This covers you, the insured members of your household, and your passengers for bodily/personal injuries, damages, or death caused by an at-fault driver who doesn't have insurance or, in some states, by a hit-and-run driver. This coverage also typically protects you and those insured under your policy when riding in someone else's car, riding a bike, or walking as a pedestrian.

Not all states require this specific coverage, but you put yourself at financial risk if you don't have it. Without uninsured motorist coverage, you could end up paying for medical bills or vehicle repairs out of your own pocket if you're in an accident with an underinsured or uninsured motorist.

Good coverage typically matches the amount of your liability coverage (see number 9).

☐ All good

☐ Needs updating

Note: _____

7. **Address:** You want to be sure that your insurance knows how to find you! Make sure your address is correct in their records. Also of great importance: Your zip code should be accurate as it can have a huge impact on how much you pay for insurance.

☐ All good

☐ Needs updating

Note: _____

8. **Annual mileage:** Your policy cost will be based in part on your annual mileage. When you first get coverage, you'll likely have to make a guesstimate of what this figure is. When you are asked for an updated mileage figure (upon renewal or sooner), be sure to report an accurate number so that your policy cost is correct. I keep track by taking a picture of my mileage every New Year. You can make it a birthday tradition too. The Consumer Federation of America (CFA) found that drivers could save an average of 5% to 10% on their car insurance rates if they reduced their annual mileage.

☐ All good

☐ Needs updating

Note: _____

9. **Liability coverage:** Make sure you have enough liability coverage if a person hits you and their policy doesn't cover your car. The most commonly required liability limits are $25,000/$50,000/$25,000, which means:

   - $25,000 in bodily injury per person
   - $50,000 in total bodily injury per accident
   - $25,000 for property damage per accident

   However, your state or your lender (if you're leasing your vehicle) might have different limits. Again, it's smart to aim for these policies to be at or above your net worth.

☐ All good

☐ Needs updating

   Note: _____

Homeowner's Insurance

Homeowner's insurance isn't legally required unless you borrow money from a mortgage lender and the terms of the loan require you to have it (which they usually do). But really, you would be crazy not to have it because it covers everything from damage from a fire to your dog biting someone outside your home and almost everything in between.

How It Works

Homeowner's insurance will protect you if a covered event damages or destroys your property or belongings. It can also cover you if an injury occurs on your property and the injured individual sues you for the related expenses.

How the Cost Is Determined

Insurers will use several factors to determine the cost of your policy, including those that will help them best determine the risk of potential payout. These factors can include:

- The age of your home
- The location of your home—is it in a flood or fire zone? Is it in a populated area?
- The home's electrical and plumbing systems
- Any renovations/upgrades
- Past claims
- Your credit history—yep, this too can impact the pricing of your policy!
- The amount of coverage and how much your deductible is

Types of Home Insurance

There are eight types of homeowner's insurance, which vary based on the type of property being insured, such as a house, condo, or mobile home, and the type of "peril" (any event, situation, or incident that causes property damage or loss) covered. The types are numbered 1 through 8, and you might see them described as "HO-1," "HO-2," "HO-3," and so on.

The most common and general types of homeowner's insurance cover things such as fire and break-ins, but perils like floods and earthquakes are often excluded. To protect yourself against these events, you would need to purchase what's referred to as an endorsement or a rider, which is basically a separate policy that adds, deletes, excludes, or changes insurance coverage.

You can get a rider for just about anything valuable you own, and it's an advised add-on if you have anything like expensive jewelry or artwork since the standard cap on coverage of these types of items is pretty low.

TIFFANY TIP: If you are a renter, you need coverage too! While a property owner's policy may cover the loss or damage of your belongings due to a fire, flood, or break-in, there's no guarantee that it will be enough—and you don't want to rely on someone else to have all their insurance ducks in a row. A renter's insurance policy will not only allow you to personalize your coverage, it will also ensure that you have the cost of temporary lodging covered should something happen to the home you're living in. You can get a renter's insurance policy relatively cheap, so don't wait—check out the tool kit for resources that will help you shop for policies today.

DO THE WORK ·······················➤

The key with homeowner's insurance is to make sure (1) you have coverage, (2) your coverage is current, and (3) you have enough coverage. To check the details of a homeowner's insurance policy, you will want to review the declaration page (usually accessible in your online account) or the preliminary policy document that's provided as you collect quotes. Here's what will appear on the declaration page, and what to check for:

1. **Name of Insured:** This will include the names of anyone insured under the policy. If you are in an unmarried partnership, be sure each person is listed separately to ensure coverage.
   ☐ All good
   ☐ Needs updating
   Note: _____

2. **Policy Period:** This will include the "effective date" and "expiration date." Start by making sure your policy is current!

☐ All good

☐ Needs updating

Note: _____

3. **Other Parties Involved:** This will include the name of your insurance agent and the company providing the insurance as well as the lender (listed as loss payee, if you have a mortgage on the property being insured).

☐ All good

☐ Needs updating

Note: _____

4. **Deductible:** The amount you are responsible for when you file a claim.

☐ All good

☐ Needs updating

Note: _____

5. **Coverage Amounts:** These will likely be broken out into five or six different categories, including dwelling, other structures, personal property, loss of use, personal liability, and medical payments to others.

☐ All good

☐ Needs updating

Note: _____

6. **Liability Limits:** These show what is covered and the maximum amount that will be paid out under each type of claim. If you see two numbers here, the first number usually shows the coverage per accident and the second the total coverage for the year.

☐ All good

☐ Needs updating

Note: _____

7. **Discounts Applied:** You may get discounts from your insurer if you have protective devices in the home such as a security system or centralized fire alarm. You can also get a discount if you bundle different types of insurance with one company.

☐ All good

☐ Needs updating

Note: _____

If you're unsure of how to make sense of all the details in a declaration page, contact your insurance agent to help you get clear on anything that's confusing. If you need help finding an agent or additional resources on homeowner's insurance, use the up-to-date list in the online tool kit for help!

The Get Good with Insurance Review

All right, you are now bursting with more information on insurance than you ever thought possible—I'm so proud of you! You know that insurance is one of the best tools for protecting you against risk, and you are ready to check your current coverage for health, life, disability, and P&C insurance.

One extra-credit item that I love is to get all the policies you have and put them in a fireproof bag. I just did this for myself, and it's such a relief to know that all these important documents are in one indestructible place. You're going to need the bag later too for the estate-planning chapter. See the tool kit for a link to the fireproof bag I have and love.

70% FINANCIALLY WHOLE

With the completion of this chapter, you are 70% financially whole! Woot! Woot!

CHAPTER 9

80% Whole
Grow Rich*ish* (Increase Your Net Worth)

A lot of people like to google the name of a favorite celebrity + "net worth" to see what kind of cash pool they might be swimming in (I am "a lot of people"). Yet these same people probably don't know what net worth really means or what their own calculation looks like. It's time we change this! Because net worth isn't a term that's relevant only to the rich—it's a free and valuable tool that everyone can use to keep tabs on their financial health and wholeness.

The Plan to Grow Your Net Worth

The goal in this chapter is to understand the concept of net worth and know how to calculate your own; to create a net worth goal and the action steps that will help you achieve it. There are four steps to this process:

1. Get to know the meaning of "net worth"—and calculate your own!
2. Accept your net worth (for now).

3. Establish your net worth goal and identify the steps you can take to meet it.

4. Make financial decisions with your net worth in mind.

WHAT YOU'LL NEED

✓ Account balances: savings, credit card, student loan, mortgage

✓ A list of what you owe and how much

✓ Most recent statements from investment accounts, including current market value

✓ A list of what you own and their financial value

Increase Your Net Worth Step 1: Get to Know the Meaning of "Net Worth"—and Calculate Your Own!

Net worth is the number you get when you subtract what you owe from what you own. Net worth *isn't* a number that says anything about what kind of person you are or what kind of personal accomplishments you've had in your life. Got it? Good. I want that to be super clear before we get into the work!

Now let's take a closer look at the net worth calculation. What you own is more formally referred to as your assets, and what you owe are considered your liabilities.

Your assets (what you own) – your liabilities (what you owe) = your net worth.

I know it likely seems kind of abstract right now, but this simple calculation will generate an important number. All you have to do is plug in your asset and liability figures, and then do some basic math to get your number. The number you get can be positive, negative, or even a zero—although it's rare for your assets and liabilities to cancel each other out.

The key to calculating your net worth accurately is to make sure you've considered *all* your assets and liabilities in your tally. Let's review what falls into each category so you know exactly what numbers to gather.

Assets	Liabilities
Savings (doesn't include checking account)	Credit card balances (that aren't paid off monthly)
*Car(s) (most cars are worth less the older they get)	*Car loan(s)
*Real estate (the value): residential, commercial, or undeveloped land	*Mortgage (current balance)
Stocks	Student loan(s)
Jewelry, art, collectibles	Personal loan balances
Precious metals	
Equipment	

* You might own and owe on some items, such as a car or a home. In these instances, the loan balances will be subtracted from the value to give you the figure that contributes to your net worth.

If you have a spouse and you are wondering if you should count any of their separate assets or liabilities, the answer is you can, but you don't have to. It's kind of like deciding if you want to file your taxes jointly or separately. Of course, if you have assets and liabilities you acquired jointly, half of those belong to you regardless of how you think about them. With those items, use a number that represents 50% of what's owed or owned in your calculation (if you decide to calculate your net worth separate from your spouse's).

If you really want to get detailed, you can calculate your net worth three ways:

1. Partnership net worth—both parties' assets and liabilities combined
2. Separate but joint net worth—your net worth combined with 50% of what's owed or owned jointly
3. Separate net worth—your net worth without including anything that's yours together (if you are married but have kept your assets and liabilities separate all along, this would be your calculation)

Keep in mind that however and whenever you decide to calculate your net worth, you are doing it for yourself. Net worth isn't like a credit score that you'll need to include on applications; it's a number that's just for you to use as a way to check in on and improve your financial health.

DO THE WORK ·····················➤

Use the Net Worth Worksheet to start gathering your asset and liability info. You can also access an online version in the tool kit at madewholeworkbook.com.

NET WORTH WORKSHEET

Complete each category by entering a value for assets and subtracting any liabilities. The difference will be your net worth.

ASSETS	VALUE		LIABILITIES	BALANCE
PERSONAL POSSESSIONS			DEBTS	
SAVING & INVESTMENTS				
RETIREMENT SAVINGS				
			TOTAL LIABILITIES:	
			TOTAL ASSETS	
			TOTAL LIABILITIES	
TOTAL ASSETS:			TOTAL NET WORTH:	

Increase Your Net Worth Step 2: Accept Your Net Worth (for Now)

This is more of a checking-in step than anything else—me checking in on you and me encouraging *you* to check in on you. The reason this is important is that sometimes seeing your total net worth can bring up some feelings, and they're not always the good kind of feelings.

Here's the truth: Whatever your net worth is, it's OK. All you have now is a number that gives you something to work with, a point of focus around which you can build your future financial actions.

DO THE WORK ·····················➤

How did you feel about seeing your net worth? Get your thoughts out of your head and down on paper. Use the space below to write out what you're thinking and feeling. If you need more than just a journal session to work through it, reach out to your accountability partner to chat about what's come up for you as it relates to your net worth.

_____

_____

_____

_____

_____

_____

IRL STORY: LISA, PORTSMOUTH, VA

Before calculating my net worth, I was just kind of living by default without any real understanding of my assets and liabilities. I had no motivation to obtain the actual number or take any deliberate steps to benefit myself or my family. And honestly, I hesitated to do the calculation because I didn't want to know if I had a negative net worth. But I wanted to work on providing a legacy of wealth for my descendants, and I realized that knowing my net worth had to be part of that work.

It was really helpful for me to hear from Tiffany that my net worth is simply a measure of my financial health, that it does not reflect on me as a person, or on my income or abilities. That made it easier to accept it for what it was.

I also appreciated discovering that I have all kinds of opportunities to change my net worth, and establishing a goal has helped me start to take advantage of those opportunities.

I am now taking purposeful steps to increase my net worth: I practice mindful spending and savings habits (I used to buy stuff I liked, but now I'm leaning toward my "needs" and "loves"); I set aside one day a week to monitor my money; I use a money program that helps me with my budget and spending and savings goals; I've set up my four basic accounts that are semi-automated; I will pay off all my credit card debt (with 0% interest rates) this year via a payment plan I have put in place, and I will use that money to feed my emergency savings account and do a bit of investing. I have a plan, and I am seeing growth. It's so rewarding, and it feels good to be in control of my money.

Increase Your Net Worth Step 3: Establish Your Net Worth Goal and Identify the Steps You Can Take to Meet It

Now that you know and accept your current net worth, let's talk about how you can increase it and get it to a positive number. A positive net worth can give you some financial breathing room, the kind that comes with peace of mind about money matters as you move through life. This is a truly priceless gift you can give yourself, which is why I encourage you to make it a goal of yours.

Aiming to achieve or increase a positive net worth isn't the same as simply trying to get a lot of money. You could make more than $1 million a year and owe $3 million. There might be more zeros in that calculation, but it would still equal a negative. You can do better with your goal.

Here's the net worth goal I encourage: to own a little bit more every single year, or to owe a little bit less every single year, or both. This is a solid goal template that can be customized by you—and that's where your work comes in!

How to Customize Your Net Worth Goal

I want you to customize your net worth goal by making it specific, realistic, and supported by action steps.

To make your goal *specific*, you need to set an amount and/or time frame. To make it *realistic*, you want to reach for the sky but make sure you aren't setting yourself up for disappointment. To make it *supported*, you want to establish some clear, doable action steps.

Here are a couple of examples of how this might look.

LAYLA'S PLAN
Specific goal: *To have a net worth of $50,000 in two years.*
Realistic goal: *I am starting with a net worth of $15,000, so this seems doable in light of my supporting actions.*

Potential action steps:

1. I will pay down my $7,000 credit card debt using the Snowball Method from the debt chapter.

2. I'm in the process of interviewing for a new job. I will negotiate a salary increase using the tips from page 117.

3. My grandmother recently passed away and left me a number of collectibles via a trust. Their estimated value is around $15,000. I will look into selling them via an auction and putting the proceeds into the market.

4. I will start my organization business. I had a few posts go viral on social media, and as a result, I have a number of clients lined up. I estimate I can make at least an additional $10,000 a year.

ADAEZE'S PLAN

Specific goal: *To increase my net worth by $100,000 within five years.*

Realistic goal: *I am starting with a net worth of negative $50,000, but a $150,000 total increase still seems doable given my supporting actions.*

Potential action steps:

1. I owe $35,000 in student loan debt but recently found out I qualify for a federal forgiveness program that will pay off my balance!

2. I will use some of the money I was using to pay off my student loans to pay off the rest of my car loan, $5,000 this year.

3. I will use the rest of my student loan payment money to pay off my $10,000 credit card debt over the next three years using the Avalanche Method in the debt chapter.

4. I earned a new certification and was able to find a new job. I negotiated a $50,000 salary increase and a $30,000 sign-on bonus.

5. I plan on using my sign-on bonus to put a down payment on a multifamily home. This will allow my tenants to pay my mortgage, allow me to save the $2,500/month I was paying in rent, and make an additional $700 per month on the property.

Now it's your turn! Don't be afraid to use the Net Worth Cheat Sheet to guide you to different chapters in the book that may help you in your goal setting.

_____'s [insert your name] Net Worth Goal Plan

Decide whether you want to focus on liabilities, assets, or both. Get specific by defining an amount and/or time frame.

My specific goal is:

_____

_____

If you've already worked your way through some of the previous chapters, you've established plans related to budgeting, savings, and debt that can help you set a realistic net worth goal. Ask yourself these questions: "Can I pay down my credit card debt to help decrease my liabilities more? Can I build my savings up more to boost my assets?" Use this close study to help you get real with your goal.

My realistic goal is:

_____

_____

Take a step back to look at your life through the lens of financial wholeness to see what steps can be implemented to help you make progress toward your net worth goal. Think about any side-hustle income you might be adding to your life or a plan in process to boost your credit score, which will allow you to refinance into a lower rate on your mortgage. Consider the raise you'll get when you present your brag book to your boss. All these forward movements, both those already in progress and those queued up for the future, should be documented here as action steps.

_____'s [insert your name] Potential Action Steps:

1. _____

2. _____

3. _____

4. _____

NET WORTH CHEAT SHEET

Increase Your Assets by:

Establishing a budget—see chapter 2

Boosting savings—see chapter 3

Earning more money—see chapter 6

Negotiating for raises—see chapter 6

Starting a side hustle—see chapter 6

Starting to invest—see chapter 7

Decrease Your Liabilities by:

Restructuring your debt—see chapter 4

Creating a debt paydown plan—see chapter 4

Using unexpected money to pay down debt faster—see chapter 4

Managing your credit—see chapter 5

Protecting what you earn—see chapter 8

Increase Your Net Worth Step 4: Make Financial Decisions with Your Net Worth in Mind

You could set yourself up with a net worth goal that's specific, realistic, and supported by action steps, and then wipe out all your work pretty swiftly if you fall back into spending habits that don't aid your progress. I'm not saying this is what's going to happen; I'm just encouraging you to carry your best intentions with you as you operate in a world that is always tempting us to spend more money.

One specific way you can protect your net worth goal is to prevent yourself from accumulating any unnecessary liabilities. This means turning down financing offers that might seem appealing at first but aren't as attractive when you think of them being added to the "what you owe" column.

This isn't to say you have to stop spending, but just be smarter about it. Instead of letting that new credit card balance build up your liabilities, increase your savings as needed so that you can pay for whatever item you were interested in without putting it on your credit card. We've gotten used to getting what we want right now by borrowing money, but patience can really pay off if you practice it.

Financing can be useful if you're buying a house, paying for healthcare or education, or purchasing a vehicle. If you avoid using it much in other areas, you will give your net worth the opportunity to grow. This is especially true of burdensome credit balances that don't get paid off monthly.

DO THE WORK ·······························➤

Keep your net worth in mind as you navigate the world, which is filled with so many ways to spend without paying attention. Seriously, you can just "tap" away hundreds of dollars a day if you're not paying attention.

Take the Protect My Net Worth Pledge

I will remember my net worth goal when I'm out in the world (or even at home on my couch shopping online). I will practice patience and spend with strategy rather than a swipe.

_____

[Signature]

The Grow Rich*ish* Review

Your net worth is a number you get when you subtract what you owe (liabilities) from what you own (assets). It doesn't reflect your income, but a positive net worth can represent peace of mind with money.

No one should ever confuse net worth with personal worth. It's a number, not a judgment. Use your net worth as a starting point around which you build strategic and specific goals to help boost your financial health.

Once you have your goals in place, be sure to revisit them every six to twelve months.

80% FINANCIALLY WHOLE

You. Are. 80%. Financially. Whole. This is big! Congratulations on all the work you've done to get this far.

CHAPTER 10

90% Whole
Pick Your Money Team
(Financial Professionals)

Here's something that might surprise you: Getting good with money is a team sport. Yep, you aren't supposed to do it alone. Yet I know most people get tossed into adulthood with little to no financial education, and few are taught about the teammates, aka financial professionals, who are out there just waiting to offer support and guidance.

The good news is that I—Teacher Tiffany—am here to introduce you to the players you might need on your team to help you get financially whole. Your specific needs will vary based on the complexity of your financial profile. If you own a business and employ others, you likely need a bookkeeper or accountant. If you have a 401(k) and modest savings, you can likely lean on a financial educator (you know, someone like me!). And regardless of your situation, you will benefit from an accountability partner.

In this chapter, you'll get to know the five most common money team members and get help figuring out who you might need most in your financial life.

The Plan to Pick Your Money Team

The goal here is to assemble a money team that will help you reach your financial goals. The steps for that are straightforward. Phew! You will learn about the following people who can support you in your pursuit of financial wholeness:

1. An accountability partner
2. A certified financial planner (CFP) or financial adviser
3. An accountant or certified public accountant (CPA)
4. An estate-planning attorney
5. An insurance broker

WHAT YOU'LL NEED

✓ The My So-Called Financial Life template
✓ Access to my Dream Catcher group

Pick Your Money Team Step 1: Get an Accountability Partner

The other money team members listed above are optional, but *everyone* needs an accountability partner. This is a person (or people—there's no harm in having more than one!) who can help keep you on track with your goals and whom you will help in the same way. It's like having a workout buddy who texts, "See you at the gym!," but instead they're your financial wholeness buddy who calls to ask how far you've moved your credit score up or if your acorn stash is growing in your emergency savings.

Now, let's be honest—there are only certain people in our lives from whom we can hear stuff like this without getting annoyed or defensive. Which is why you want to be selective about whom you approach to be your accountability partner. You want it to be someone who is supportive and encouraging, and someone who is not overly opinionated about your choices. You don't want to invite judgment; you want to invite and extend positive, uplifting support.

For me, the ideal accountability partner is a Dream Catcher. This is the term I use for people who are empowering and supportive, and who are focused on and excited about financial growth. (If this sounds like a unicorn to you, I've created a private group of the same name where many people who share these qualities have connected and united.)

Do you have any Dream Catchers in your life? The best way to attract a Dream Catcher is to be a Dream Catcher!

DO THE WORK ┈┈┈┈┈┈┈➤

What characteristics do you think would be most helpful to you in an accountability partner? I shared adjectives like supportive and encouraging, but your ideal person might have different qualities. Do you need someone who's extra compassionate and sensitive? Or maybe someone who's tough and persistent? Write down a few adjectives here.

The ideal qualities for my accountability partner are:

_____

_____

_____

Now think of someone in your life who has some of these qualities, whom you would also feel comfortable talking to about money matters. This might be your mom or sibling, or a best friend or coworker. Got someone or a few people in mind? OK, good. Write their names down (if you want; you can also keep it in your head if you'd rather).

Possible accountability partners:

_____

_____

_____

Next, consider what kind of support would be most helpful to you. Do you want to connect weekly or monthly? Do you want to get on the phone or meet in person? Do you want to share Google docs? Jot down some ideas on how you envision your accountability partnership working.

How and how often do I want to have check-ins with my accountability partner?

_____

_____

_____

Now it's time to ask your accountability partner if they want to join forces. Don't stress over the script; simply say, "Hey, do you want to help keep each other on track as we work toward achieving our financial goals?" I hope that it's a match and that you help elevate each other.

If you can't find a good fit in your inner circle, I encourage you to join my Dream Catcher community and ask someone there for support. The Dream Catcher community is filled with amazing people who spend a lot of time lifting one another up; I know they will welcome you with open arms! Join us and find your financial bestie via the link in the online tool kit (madewholeworkbook.com).

Pick Your Money Team Step 2: Consider a Certified Financial Planner or a Financial Adviser

A certified financial planner is a professional who can look at your financial assets and help align your actions with your financial goals. Because of their educational background, they can help you navigate through most areas related to financial wholeness, including budgeting, debt management, retirement, college financial planning, estate planning, tax planning, and risk management. And because of this breadth of knowledge, if they do join your money team, they'll be the most likely to play team captain and help you select other professionals.

> **TIFFANY TIP:** As the job title suggests, a certified financial planner has to be certified—they have to pass a certification exam—and they are held by their industry to high ethical standards. You can verify a CFP's credentials at finra.org.

Not everyone needs a financial planner or adviser. Whether or not you need one will be based on your income, profession, and assets. Here are some questions to help you assess if you need one (circle either yes or no):

1. Are you in school for a specialty career (e.g., as a doctor or lawyer) that might earn you a lot of money right out of school? Yes/No
2. Are you close to retirement and haven't yet met with a financial planner or adviser? Yes/No
3. Have you come into a significant amount of money ($50,000 or more) from an inheritance, sign-on bonus, or property sale? Yes/No
4. Has your financial life become more complicated due to an increase in assets? For example, the purchase of one or more properties, or starting a business. Yes/No

If you answered yes to any of the above questions, you could benefit from the guidance offered by a CFP. But only if you're ready to share *all* the details of your financial life. You've got to be prepared to hand over bank statements, retirement info, insurance info, details on your credit history, and more. If this makes you squirm, you may not be ready, and you should consider spilling all the beans to your accountability buddy first!

If and when you feel you're ready to search for a financial planner or financial adviser, I recommend you prioritize two specific criteria as you compare your options.

1. Compensation: The fees paid for financial advice can vary widely because there are a few different ways that a financial planner may be paid. The payment structure might be one of the following:

- **Fee-only,** which means they are paid directly by you for their services to you. You might pay them a flat fee per transaction, an hourly rate for the time they put into helping manage your finances, a yearly retainer (a flat fee for the year), or a percentage of assets under management (referred to as AUM). A fee-only adviser does not collect commissions through any products they recommend to clients, and they are what's referred to as a fiduciary, which means they are legally obligated to put their clients' interests ahead of their own. If you choose to pay based on a percentage, know that the average is 1%, but you should negotiate.
- **Fee-based** advisers get paid by you, the client, but they also can get paid through commissions on insurance or mutual funds or other types of financial products they might sell you.
- **Commission-based** advisers are paid only through the commissions they make on products they sell you (meaning you don't pay them a separate fee). While this type of adviser can be a fiduciary, they don't have to be.

My recommendation: If you've determined that you do need a CFP, opt for the fee-only kind. This approach gives you payment options (flat fee, hourly, retainer, etc.)

and eliminates the worry that your adviser might try to sell you financial products you don't need because they'll make a commission on those sales.

If you want to hire an adviser but find it is cost prohibitive, consider a robo-adviser. A robo-adviser is a form of financial guidance based on an algorithm. You still get personalized management by completing a questionnaire, but the service comes at around half the cost of a traditional adviser. See the online tool kit for an up-to-date list of some of my top robo-adviser options.

2. Personality fit: You're going to need to share a lot of information with your financial planner, and this is easier to do if you *like* the person you hire. I'm not saying they have to be in the running for your BFF, but they should be someone whose personality seems to work well with your own.

One way to gauge for fit is to narrow your choices down to a few potential advisers and then—before arranging for a time to interview them—share with them a detailed look at your financial profile, some information about your personality, and your goals. With these details in hand, they will have a good understanding of what you need and want from them, and they should be able to tailor their advice to you accordingly.

When I was looking for a CFP, I shared with candidates a document I created and completed called My So-Called Financial Life. I was super specific, and this made it clear that I was super serious about my money. I knew the level of detail would scare a few off but hoped the right person would show up—and she did!

DO THE WORK ·····················➤

- Figure out if you should consider adding a financial planner/adviser to your money team by answering the questions on page 217.
- If an adviser could be beneficial to you, start searching for a good fit. Begin by asking family and friends for a recommendation. You can also reach out to the Dream Catcher group and visit the tool kit to see a current list of suggested sites that will be helpful. Make note of any potential candidates below:

_____

_____

_____

- To help get a clear picture of your financial profile and your goals, fill out the My So-Called Financial Life template below. This will help you get clear on what you want and need and will be a good document to share with potential CFP candidates before interviewing them.

MY SO-CALLED FINANCIAL LIFE TEMPLATE

You can also access this template in the online tool kit at madewholework book.com.

What I'm looking for:

_____

_____

_____

Example: I want to use my money to match my values and to fund a great life. I'd like to pay (hourly or annually) for advice on how to best do so. I want help creating a retirement plan and a plan to pay for college and to support my special-needs child when I'm no longer here.

Current (Financial) Situation:

- Age, marital status, children:

_____

- Employment:

_____

- Homeownership? Renting?

_____

- Cars? What's owed?

_____

- Debt: Student loans, credit cards. Balances? Current status? Current? Behind?

_____

- Credit scores:

_____

- Retirement accounts: A pension? IRA? 401(k)? Roth IRA? How much? Are there any loans withdrawn? What companies manage them?

_____

- Individual stocks? How much do you have invested? What platform are you using?

_____

- Other investments: Real estate? Other investment accounts? Value?

_____

- Insurance: Do you have disability, pet, homeowner's, renter's, health, term life, whole life? How much? With which companies? Does your job offer health/disability/life insurance? How much? Does your spouse or child have insurance? How much?

_____

- How much does it cost to maintain yourself and your family for a month?

_____

- How much was your adjusted gross household income for last year? (Check your tax return.)

_____

- I currently have in savings:

_____

- I would say I: Am fairly frugal? Spend too much? Moderate?

_____

- Any business? List any gross business income from last year. What kind of business? LLC? S corporation? C corporation? Do you have a business partner? What percentage do you own?

_____

Pick Your Money Team Step 3: Consider an Accountant

An accountant is a finance professional who specializes in tax planning and can assist you in finding ways to minimize your tax burden. You really only need an accountant on your money team if you have a complex tax profile.

Here are some questions to help you identify whether or not you need an accountant (circle either yes or no):

1. Do you own a business or businesses? Yes/No
2. Do you own property or multiple properties? Yes/No
3. Are you concerned about upcoming tax deadlines? Yes/No
4. Are you being audited? Yes/No
5. Is your business growing quickly? Yes/No

If you answered yes to any of the above questions, you may benefit from hiring an accountant. When you're ready to search for an accountant, these are the factors you want to consider.

- **Type of accountant:** There are accountants and there are certified public accountants, otherwise known as CPAs. Ideally, you will want to hire a CPA as they have met state licensing requirements, and they're allowed to represent taxpayers during IRS audits.
- **Fees:** Typically, CPAs will charge either by the hour or a flat fee for tax filing services. Be sure to ask about this up front.
- **Services:** CPAs can file your taxes, identify how you can reduce your tax burden, and advise on financial planning throughout the year. Think about what services you might need and make sure the person you're considering can meet your needs.
- **Specialty:** If you work in a specialized field or need a specific type of tax advice, make sure you look for someone who has experience with your specific needs.

- **Identification status:** The IRS issues a preparer tax identification number (PTIN) to CPAs. Check irs.gov to make sure the CPA you are considering working with is registered in this way.

DO THE WORK ··························➤

- Figure out if you should consider adding a financial planner/adviser to your money team by answering the questions on page 217.
- If a CPA could be beneficial to you, start searching for a good fit. As with the financial planner search, I suggest you begin by asking family and friends for a recommendation. Make note of any potential candidates below, and include any information you gather about pricing or how they work:

_____

_____

_____

IRL STORY: SHIRLEY, BRONX, NY

Before getting serious about my future, I walked around like, "I don't have money, so I'm not paying attention to it." This led to my making money mistakes—not maximizing on 401(k) accounts, not saving in alternate sources—and forgetting the standards that my mom showed me over the years. When I realized that retirement was in view, I knew I needed to do better and figure out how I wanted to live in that next phase.

That's where learning how to assemble a money team has helped me. I appreciated Tiffany's advice to stick with people you trust who will tell you the truth. I had a long-standing relationship with a couple of certified financial planners through union partnerships. Since I was able to get to know them as people first, there was an enhanced level of trust. This allowed me to "get my ducks in a row"—to learn how my funds would work for me, set limits that differed from how I operated in the working world, and breathe just a little bit so I could plot my next moves.

I was also fortunate to find a great tax man! He has been able to make taxes very clear to me so I can now go into situations and make the best decisions for my future and that of my children. You never know how important it is to have this person in your corner.

It's helpful to know I have these professionals to support me along the way and to "slap my hand" if I'm exhibiting old money behaviors. I am still a work in progress, and I need that from time to time. Because I have good financial professionals working for me, I know I'm on the right track now for myself and my family.

Pick Your Money Team Step 4: Consider an Estate-Planning Attorney

An estate-planning attorney specializes in helping people create legal documents such as a will, trust, and power of attorney, and they can counsel you in the areas of inheritance tax, asset protection, and family preservation (i.e., ensuring that guardianship terms are clearly and legal defined). Ultimately, what an estate-planning attorney does is help to make sure your wishes are legally enforceable should you become incapacitated or die.

Here are some questions to help you identify whether or not you need an estate-planning attorney (circle either yes or no):

1. Do you have a large or blended family? Yes/No
2. Do you have children who are minors or family members with special needs, or other dependents? Yes/No
3. Can you think of a family member who might contest your will? Yes/No

4. Do you own a family business or investment properties? Yes/No
5. Do you want to create a trust? Yes/No
6. Do you have assets in other states or countries? Yes/No
7. Are you worried about estate or inheritance taxes? Yes/No

If you answered yes to any of the above questions, you may benefit from hiring an estate attorney. When you're ready to search for one, these are the factors you want to consider.

- **Reputation:** Because of the serious nature of estate matters, you want to make sure you hire someone who is experienced enough to have generated plenty of positive reviews. It's best to try to get a personal referral, so don't be afraid to ask around. You want to hire someone who is thorough and professional while also still sensitive to the fact that discussing life-and-death matters can be a little unsettling.
- **Areas of expertise:** Some estate attorneys are great with drawing up trusts to protect your assets; others may focus on assisting clients with establishing complicated guardianship nomination terms. It can be helpful to work with an attorney who is experienced in whatever specific area you may need legal guidance in. It's also important to make sure they are in fact an estate-planning attorney rather than a general attorney.
- **Cost:** The cost for services varies widely, but you want to make sure you know up front how much you'll be expected to pay. If your initial research suggests that an estate attorney might be beyond your budget, be sure to check out the tool kit for some reputable online options.

DO THE WORK ·······················➤

- Figure out if you should consider adding an estate-planning attorney to your money team by answering the questions on page 225. You might also know more about your needs after you work through the estate-planning chapter, which is up next in our pursuit of financial wholeness.

- If an estate-planning attorney could be beneficial to you, start searching for a good fit. A word-of-mouth referral is best, so don't be afraid to ask around. Make note of any potential candidates below, and include any information you gather about pricing or how they work:

_____

_____

_____

_____

_____

_____

_____

_____

_____

Pick Your Money Team Step 5: Consider an Insurance Broker

An insurance broker can help you purchase policies for any type of insurance, including home, auto, pet, health, and life. A broker is different from an insurance agent in that they work for *you*, whereas an agent represents one or more insurance companies.

Here are some questions to help you identify whether or not you need an insurance broker (circle either yes or no):

1. Are you underinsured in one or more areas but can't find the time to shop for the coverage you need? Yes/No
2. Are you working with an insurance agent who you feel isn't providing customized service or protecting your best interests? Yes/No
3. Do you think your insurance situation requires specialized assistance? Yes/No

If you answered yes to any of the above questions, you may benefit from hiring an insurance broker. When you're ready to search for one, these are the factors you want to consider:

- **Depth of knowledge:** Insurance can be extremely nuanced, so you want to work with someone who gets the ins and outs of policies and can ensure that you have sufficient coverage, which is a calculation unique to you.
- **Fiduciary status:** Some brokers have a fiduciary duty to the client *and* the company they represent, which means their product recommendations might not be made only in your best interest. Ask the broker directly if they are a fiduciary so you can make an informed decision about whether to work with them.
- **Licensing:** Both insurance agents and brokers have to be licensed by their state before selling to the public. You will want to make sure the broker you are interested in working with has a license and that it's up to date. A quick Google search will pull up your state's license look-up site.

DO THE WORK ┄┄┄┄┄┄┄➤

- Figure out if you should consider adding an insurance broker to your money team by answering the questions on page 227. If you need to revisit your specific insurance needs, jump back to the insurance chapter to see if you might be underinsured in one or more areas.

- If an insurance broker could be beneficial to you, start searching for a good fit. Ask your friends and family if they know any good insurance brokers in your area. Make note of any potential candidates below, and include any questions you may have on how the process works and how much their services cost:

_____

_____

_____

_____

_____

_____

_____

The Pick Your Money Team Review

We covered the five key players on your money team:

1. An accountability partner
2. A certified financial planner or financial adviser
3. An accountant or CPA
4. An estate-planning attorney
5. An insurance broker

We also covered the fact that the only one on this list that I consider mandatory for everyone is the accountability partner. That's the person with whom you can talk about your financial goals and how you're going to achieve them, and who can help keep you on track (and vice versa!).

The rest of your money teammates are optional and dependent on your professional or financial circumstances. Don't underestimate the power of surrounding yourself with the right team when it comes to your money. And be sure to do your due diligence before handing over your personal information to just anyone. Any time you invest up front will be worth it!

90% FINANCIALLY WHOLE

Yes, you have reached 90% financial wholeness. You can't see me now, but I'm beaming with pride! And you should be too.

CHAPTER 11

100% Whole
Leave a Legacy
(Estate Planning)

An estate plan is a plan for what happens to you, your property, your dependents, and your assets when you become incapacitated or pass away. It's a big deal, but it can become an even bigger ordeal for the people you love most if you don't deal with it.

If you haven't established an estate plan, you're not alone. According to a 2022 survey, 67% of people living in the United States do not have an estate plan. This means that more than half the population is leaving some major after-life decisions to others. At the end of the day, that's all an estate plan is: a collection of decisions that will allow for your wishes to live on past you.

Some of you reading this might be thinking, *I don't have any kind of "estate," so none of this applies to me.* Yet the term "estate" really means anything that belongs to you. This could be your dog, your clothes, your car, your jewelry, and, yes, your kid(s). When you have a plan for your property and anyone you take care of, your loved ones are given the gift of being able to grieve without having to fight with one another or fix problems or figure things out on your behalf when you're no longer around.

It's especially important that you have a plan in place if your estate is more complex, which is the case if you own property or other sizable assets, if you own a business, or if you have a blended family. And if you are a parent and don't have a guardianship plan in place, you owe it to your child or children to get a plan notarized like *right now*.

At the end of the day, having an estate plan is about knowing that the choices you made will protect you and the people you love. It's about saying *I love my family so much that I'm going to do this thing that makes me a little uncomfortable.* I'll help you through it.

I Lost the Love of My Life

In 2021, I lost my husband, Jerrell Smith. It was unexpected and sudden. He died from an aneurysm at forty-one years old. To be honest, I'm still reeling from the loss. I'm crying as I type this, because I now know firsthand how important having an estate plan is. Transparently, because he and I were so "young" (I was forty-two then), we dragged our feet about getting our will and trust together. We thought we had time. Despite what I know I should have done, I was only 90% financially whole because our estate plan was incomplete.

Thankfully, the conversations we did have and our regular meetings with our financial adviser gave me clarity about most of his financial wishes. Despite that, not having a will and trust in place did cause some difficulty, both familial and financial, when trying to settle his estate.

If you're looking for a sign to work on your estate plan today, this is it. I miss my Superman so much, but because of our mostly good financial choices, I get to just mourn him and not struggle with the financial loss too. I want that for you and your family.

The Plan to Leave a Legacy

In this chapter, you're going to create and implement a plan for what will happen to your cash, real estate, jewelry, and other assets (aka, your estate) after you pass. No matter the size of your bank account and level of assets, you'll follow the same seven steps:

1. Fill out or check beneficiary forms.
2. Think about guardianship for minor children and/or a special-needs family member.
3. Write a will.
4. Deal with your advance directives, a living will and durable power of attorney.
5. Think about and document your long-term-care plan.
6. Set up a (living) trust.
7. Execute and fund these plans!

WHAT YOU'LL NEED

✓ First and foremost, an ability to set aside any fears of dying long enough to make decisions that will matter to your loved ones

✓ Some quiet time and a warm cup of tea (or something stronger, if that's *your* cup of tea) to accompany you as you contemplate your wishes

✓ A willingness to commit to doing one of the steps in this chapter every three to six months. If, however, you are a parent without a guardianship plan in place for any minor children (page 236), or a person in a relationship that's serious enough that you would want this person making decisions for you (page 243), you should act now.

✓ An estate-planning attorney. The best way to find one is to start by asking trusted friends and family members for referrals. Also consult with financial professionals with whom you work, such as accountants, insurance agents, and bankers. They may be able to refer you to attorneys they know and trust. Use the money team chapter of this book to help you.

Leave a Legacy Step 1: Fill Out or Check Beneficiary Forms

Assigning a beneficiary is the easiest part of establishing an estate plan, so we're going to start with that. A beneficiary is the person or persons who will receive your money or payout from a life insurance policy or trust if you pass away. The process of assigning or updating your designated beneficiary may be as simple as logging into an online account and filling in the name. In some cases, however, you will need to call an institution to confirm your designations, and even sign a document confirming your change.

Despite how simple this process can be, a lot of people put it off. Yet not assigning or updating your beneficiaries can lead to money getting locked up in probate or possibly worse: your money could go to the wrong person or people. Your beneficiary designation will supersede a will, which means that if an ex is your beneficiary, they are legally entitled to the money even if your current spouse or partner is the intended recipient according to your will. Read that last sentence again . . . and make sure you keep your beneficiaries up-to-date!

Here are some definitions to consider when assigning beneficiaries:

Primary beneficiary: Who will actually get the money

Secondary beneficiary: Who will get the money *only* if the primary beneficiary is no longer here

Minor children: Minor children can be beneficiaries. If they are still underage when you pass, the state will typically keep their money in a trust until they are eighteen years old.

Multiple beneficiaries: You can have more than one primary or secondary beneficiary. For example, I had my late husband, Jerrell, as my primary beneficiary and my four sisters as secondary beneficiaries with 25% of the funds going to each. You can decide on the percentages as well.

A trust as a beneficiary: A beneficiary doesn't have to be a person. You can assign a trust and even an organization like a nonprofit.

DO THE WORK ·····················➤

Check or change your beneficiary. There are three types of accounts that give you the opportunity to assign a beneficiary. These include bank accounts; retirement and investment accounts, such as 401(k)s and IRAs; and life insurance policies.

> To check your bank/high-interest savings account beneficiary, call or visit a local branch, or log into your online account to see if you can spot a "manage beneficiaries" tab.
> My bank account/s beneficiaries have been updated. ☐ Date: _____

> To check your retirement and investment accounts, connect with your HR specialist or call the adviser or institution managing your investments to see how to best update your beneficiaries.
> My retirement account beneficiaries have been updated. ☐ Date: _____

> To check your life insurance policy, contact your agent or reach out to the insurance company directly to see how to edit your beneficiaries.
> My life insurance policy beneficiary has been updated. ☐ Date: _____

> Equally important as updating your beneficiaries is letting them know you've made them yours! And placing the paperwork in a place that can be easily found

and accessed when you're not here. For example, a safe or safe-deposit box that only you can get into is not a good place to store this information.

My beneficiaries have been notified and know where my paperwork is.

☐ Date: _____

TIFFANY TIP: If you are married or in a serious partnership with someone you trust with your money, I recommend having at least one joint bank account. My husband, Jerrell, and I had joint bank accounts, and when he passed away, I was able to access and transfer money out of that account without having to jump through hoops. Otherwise, once a death is reported, the bank can legally lock that person's account, and you might not have access to it for months.

Leave a Legacy Step 2: Think About Guardianship for Minor Children and/or a Special-Needs Family Member

I think a lot of parents put off assigning a guardian because they don't like to envision a world in which they are not present in their children's lives and in charge of raising them. But just think of all the choices you have to make every single day around parenting your child or children—who would you want to make those choices for your child if something were to happen to you and their other parent? If you have a preference, as I suspect you do, it does no good if you keep it to yourself. A guardianship plan is the only way to ensure that your parenting wishes are still present even if you are not.

We will get to how you make the actual guardian appointment in the next step, but for now I encourage you to start thinking about potential guardians and prepare your co-parent for the considerations and conversations to come. (Of course, if you've already assigned a guardian and have it in your will, good for you! It's no small thing to get this decision settled.)

DO THE WORK ·····················➤

Write out your specific wishes. If you have a child or children and/or a special-needs family member, think about some of the ways you're raising or caring for them that you would want to continue if you were gone. That is, would you want them to be educated in a certain way? Or raised according to a specific religion? Do they need to be in an area that has access to a specialty type of care? This doesn't have to be an exhaustive list, but write down anything that comes to mind.

_____

_____

_____

_____

_____

Confirm your candidate and get the conversation on your calendar. Consider your options for a guardian and, if relevant, start having conversations with your parenting partner about who is on the list of potential candidates. Once you've narrowed it down, schedule a conversation with the person or people you want to ask.

When it's time to talk, it's best to present your plan plainly: "I/we would like to name you as the legal guardian of our children should something happen to me/us." And then be prepared to share any of your specific wishes that may have come up in your notes above.

Keep in mind that there's no guarantee that whomever you ask will accept the designation. Even if they feel it's an honor to be considered, they may not be prepared to take on that level of responsibility. If they say, "Thank you, but no," respect their feelings and thank them for being honest! Go back to your list and think of who might be next in line.

When you find the right person to accept the guardianship assignment, make sure to get the designation in your will. See the next step for how to get this done.

Set your plans down here to help ensure that they happen:

I've decided whom I'm going to ask to be my child's guardian: _____

_____

We are scheduled to talk on _____ [insert date].

Leave a Legacy Step 3: Write a Will

A will, which is also known as a last will and testament, is a document that will speak for you when you depart this world. Unlike a trust that can tell your family or descendants what to do with your estate years after you've passed, a will tells folks what to do immediately after you've died. It can declare any guardianship plans related to any minor children, whom you want to manage your affairs (a person referred to as the executor), what your wishes are regarding anything you owe or own, and any other specific requests you may have related to your affairs.

One of the biggest questions about wills is how old you should be when you create one. If you own property or you have children, you should have a will in place now. Other than that, you should consider writing one once you turn twenty-five. You might think that sounds really young for a will, but most of us have acquired some assets of personal significance by then.

Remember, a will is just a template, which means that your job is to fill in your wishes as you understand them at this point in your life. Your wishes may change as your life does, especially if you get married or divorced or have children, but it's much easier to go back and update a will than to get your original one drafted.

DO THE WORK ·······················➤

Think of who should be considered in your estate planning. This might be your significant other, children, siblings, parents, cousins, or close friends. Write down who comes to mind, in no particular order.

_____

_____

Think of what should be included. If you completed the Net Worth Worksheet on page 204, it will be helpful to refer to this (or return to it if it's not completed) to help you get a clear picture of what you own and owe. Spend a little more time here to make sure you've thought of everything, as some property and assets may not have immediately come to mind in the earlier exercise. These forgotten items might include:

- An insurance policy
- Profits from stocks or bonds
- Mutual funds
- Certificates of deposits (CDs)
- Proprietary products (an idea or object that only you own, like a patent, trademark, or copyright)

If you think of any property and assets that weren't included on the Net Worth Worksheet or any items that may have more sentimental than monetary value, write them down here:

_____

_____

_____

Think of the decisions that you don't want your family or loved ones to have to make on your behalf. There are decisions around death and dying that no one wants to think about, but the hard truth is that if you don't do the thinking and the deciding, you are making someone else do that work. It's a gift to take this work off their plate so that they can focus on grieving. Some questions to contemplate and answer here if you'd like:

Who is your appointed guardian for your children? (Yes, I know we've already gone over this—just making sure this is still at the top of your list.)

_____

Are you an organ donor?

_____

Do you want to be cremated or buried?

_____

Where do you want to be buried?

_____

Do you have money set aside for your final expenses?

_____

Any of these details that pertain specifically to your funeral wishes and final arrangements *can* be put in your will, but they also should be documented somewhere separate from your will.

If it's within your budget, hire an estate-planning attorney to help you get a will created. You can also utilize online resources to create a basic will, but most DIY templates won't cover more complicated matters like detailed financial scenarios or complex family dynamics. Visit the tool kit for some online resources, and revisit page 227 to see if you made notes regarding any potential estate-planning attorneys to contact.

I know it might seem like an overwhelming task to get a will done, but it doesn't have to be. Did you know that many estate-planning attorneys have template wills in place? Yes! With one phone call, you can make minor tweaks to their template and have a will ready to sign in less than twenty-four hours. Last year, I was finally able to convince my aging parents to update their over-thirty-year-old will, and we followed this formula with my attorney. And within three days, we had a signed will and we had it notarized at their bank.

Make it a priority to create your will. Getting something like your will done takes a little extra push because it's not something anyone wants to do. Get out your calendar and give yourself a deadline, something like, "I'm going to get my will details down on paper before the end of the month." Or maybe make an appointment with the attorney to create a deadline.

IRL STORY: TIFFANY, NEWARK, NJ

As I shared earlier in this chapter, I lost the love of my life, best friend, and husband, Jerrell, aka Superman, suddenly in 2021. I didn't know it at the time, but there were whispers to help me get ready. We had talked about finally getting our wills done a week before he passed away, which is still something that shakes me. Although we never completed them, we did do just about everything else to get our joint and separate financial lives in order. Because of that, when he died, I was able to just get to miss my person, and not everyone can say that. Some people lose their person *and* their house . . . and their grief is already too much. That's why we put things like wills in place; they help take care of your person and your people.

One thing I learned about losing someone is the importance of the nonfinancial things that can mean so much when they're gone. Here are some of the things that helped lift me up through some of the toughest days:

- **Videos:** Turns out Jerrell was like a secret vlogger, and I found all these videos of him on his phone just documenting little moments, like him helping my niece and nephew build a model helicopter on Christmas morning. Or him just talking about his day or saying sweet things to me. I have so many videos that I could literally find a video of him saying "I love you" whenever I needed to hear it. You don't even know what a delight it is to discover something like that during the darkest of times.

- **A Google photo album:** This free app allows you to tag someone's face in your phone and then see any images you have with them in it. If I'm having a bad day, I can go and see just about any picture of Jerrell. It's the greatest gift. You can even add family and friends to the album and tag your person's face in their phone too. My joint "Jerrell" album has thousands of videos and pictures as a result.

- **Passwords:** At least one person other than you should have the PIN/passwords for your accounts. At minimum, make sure someone has the password or access to your phone and email, since it is from these bases that they will be able to unlock any other accounts. Because Jerrell always used my computer, I had all his passwords saved in a free password management app. It made life so much easier during a difficult time.

- **Doc protector.** One of the hardest things your family will have to navigate when you're not here is hunting down all your accounts and important papers. Keep a copy of all your (bank, insurance, investment) statements and an original copy of your will in a fireproof and waterproof bag. I found mine online, and I let my sisters know where I keep it inside my home.

These might seem like small things, but they've been essential to my life since Jerrell passed away.

Leave a Legacy Step 4: Deal with Your Advance Directives, a Living Will and Durable Power of Attorney

Advance directives are instructions regarding your medical care that are put in place and used only if you become incapable of communicating how you'd like to be cared for. There are a few different types of advanced directives, but I'm going to focus on a living will and a durable power of attorney.

A **living will** is a legal document that outlines what type of medical care or intervention you would want if you were still alive but incapacitated due to injury or illness. In this document, you can specify if you'd want life-sustaining treatment, resuscitation, or intubation, and make it known if you would want to be an organ or tissue donor if you were to pass away.

You can also use your living will to designate an agent who would be in charge of making sure your wishes are followed. This agent must be someone you would literally trust with your life. (So maybe don't pick your one cousin who has a hard-core grudge against you. Kidding. Sort of. But not really. *Don't you dare pick her.*)

In some states, you will need to also legally establish this person as eligible to speak on your behalf by designating them as your healthcare power of attorney, which is equivalent to a durable power of attorney.

A **durable power of attorney** is a legal document that allows you to grant another person the authority to make decisions on your behalf if you were to become incapacitated. A durable power of attorney is different from a standard power of attorney (POA) because though the word *durable* might suggest otherwise, a durable power of attorney gives your agent power to act on your behalf only when you are unconscious or severely unwell. If you regain your health, their power is essentially revoked, and you resume control of the choices surrounding your care and life.

A durable power of attorney can be created for your healthcare decisions and for managing your finances. Some people will pick the same person to act on their behalf in these areas, while others may prefer different people in these roles.

DO THE WORK ·······················➤

Consider the people closest to you: your spouse or significant other, your siblings, adult children, or parents. Who among them would you want making sure your wishes are carried out? Once you've decided, have a conversation to ask if they would be comfortable in this role.

And let me pause here to point out that no one can really say they're "comfortable" in a role like this—the question should probably go more like, "Listen, can you keep it together if something unexpected goes down and I need you to represent me?"

These are discomforting thoughts and conversations, but you are giving a gift to those who love you when you have the roles clearly assigned and your wishes clearly documented.

I've identified my living will and POA agents and confirmed that they will speak for me if I'm ever in a position where I can't. ☐ Date: _____:

I've called my bank or other financial institutions to confirm how a durable power of attorney would need to read in order for my POA to represent me, if needed. ☐ Date: _____:

Leave a Legacy Step 5: Think About and Document Your Long-Term-Care Plan

Another important part of your estate planning is establishing a long-term-care plan. This is a plan that details how you would want to be taken care of if you were to need help with everyday activities, such as bathing, getting dressed, and eating.

I think regardless of age, we probably all would like to think that the time for this will be way off in the future, so why start planning for it now? Well, for one, you're working on your estate plan, so why not just get it done now? For another, you are likely sharper and of sounder mind than you'll be years or decades down the road. This is the version of you that you want making some decisions.

One of the primary considerations of long-term care is cost. There are two ways to prepare for the expense of long-term care. You can:

1. Check out long-term care insurance. This type of insurance is expensive, and there aren't any options on the market to get a fixed rate, but single people or people without children may decide it's a necessary expense to protect them later in life.

2. Build the cost of long-term care into your financial planning. As a way of self-insuring, you can designate specific assets to be saved for this part of your life. This is where having a certified financial planner (CFP) is helpful. My CFP, Anjali, helped me to plan and fund this part of my estate plan.

DO THE WORK ·······························➤

If you haven't had personal experience with long-term care, either through a grandparent, parent, or other older relative, it can be tough to envision your wants in this arena of later life. So it's really a creative exercise that you'll want to put your mind to sooner or later, depending on your age.

If you are over forty, start thinking about what your long-term healthcare might look like. Write down any preferences that come to mind, such as in-home support all the way or a nursing facility with plenty of community events. If you don't have a certified financial planner already, it might be useful to consider getting one at this point.

If you are over fifty, consider meeting with an attorney or talking to an insurance agent about what the potential or expected costs of long-term care in your area (or elsewhere if you plan to retire in a different locale) will be.

Lastly, let's make this activity less gloom and doom! I want you to write down the most awesome version of the life you want as an older person here. Then start to ask yourself what and whom you need to make it happen.

My Best (Later-in-Life) Life:

_____

_____

_____

_____

_____

Leave a Legacy Step 6: Set Up a (Living) Trust

There are two main legal entities you can use to dictate what can be done with your property: a will and a trust. You've hopefully already done the work of drafting the details of your will, which is something every person needs. A trust—which isn't essential for all—is different from a will in that it lets you establish what you would want to happen in perpetuity with your property and assets. It allows your wishes to be activated immediately and also lets them reach into the future to communicate exactly when and how anything you own should be distributed.

A trust will also require you to identify a trustee. This is a person who will be the legal owner of your trust assets, who will also be responsible for managing any of the assets in your trust, the tax filings for the trust, and distributing the assets according to what you've outlined in your trust. You can appoint yourself as your own trustee while you're living.

Because creating a trust takes work, time, and money—you need to hire an attorney to have one set up properly—it's important to make sure you need one before investing any of your resources. Generally, a trust isn't necessary unless you have at least $100,000 in assets. Look back at your Net Worth Worksheet to see if your assets add up to this amount or more. If so, and especially if your assets are $500,000 or more, you should seriously consider establishing a trust.

There are a few key benefits to having a trust:

- **You help your heirs avoid the probate process.** Probate is the court-supervised execution of your will. If you took the time to designate beneficiaries (jump back to step 1 in this chapter if you haven't done that yet), the probate process makes sure that your wishes are honored and that those beneficiaries get what you wanted them to get. If you didn't identify beneficiaries during your lifetime, you set up the potential for a lot of headache and heartache among your family members.

   But even if you've identified beneficiaries, the transfer of your property to your heirs (the probate process) can still be a lengthy and costly process, especially if you have a lot of assets. A trust makes the transfer easier and faster.

- **You keep your affairs private.** The probate process is public since when you die, a will becomes public record. However, if you have a trust in place, only the trustees and beneficiaries know the sum of your assets. It's definitely a more surefire way to keep people out of your business.

   The two main types of trusts are *revocable* and *irrevocable*. A **revocable trust** is the most common type of trust. This type of trust makes you the boss and allows you to make any modifications without consulting others. Changes might include selling and removing properties from your trust or modifying any of the assigned beneficiaries.

   An **irrevocable trust** is one where you can't make changes without the permission of all the affected beneficiaries (i.e., all parties identified as the beneficiaries of the property held in the trust). Since it can be difficult to get multiple beneficiaries to agree to changes, you want to be sure an irrevocable trust is right for you before setting one up. It's really only needed for people who have at least $500,000 in assets. If you have less than that and an estate attorney is recommending an irrevocable trust, I would get a second opinion.

DO THE WORK ·······················➤

Revisit the Net Worth Worksheet to check the tally of your assets. Do you see six figures there? If so, you want to consider creating a trust. If you don't see a figure of at least $100,000 yet, remember to revisit the consideration of a trust as your net worth grows.

If you've identified a preliminary need to establish a trust, refer back to page 225 on how to start your search for an estate-planning attorney. Make note here of any potential candidates:

_____

_____

Leave a Legacy Step 7: Execute and Fund These Plans!

Here's the tricky thing about estate plans—they are essentially meaningless until they are signed by you! If you've done all the work to get some of the most important documents you'll ever create in your life drafted, don't let them get stuck in limbo—because that's where your loved ones will be if something happens to you.

DO THE WORK ·······················➤

Phew, just one last stretch of effort to make sure all your estate-planning work doesn't go to waste. My estate-planning attorney, Toni Moore, shared that so many folks do all this heavy lifting to create a will and trust and never actually sign or fund them. But that won't be you. You're going to do the work.

1. Sign your will, trust, and other documents and get them notarized. One of the best places to get something notarized is your local bank. Make an appointment and go!

2. If you have a trust, fund it. That means changing the title of the home(s) you want in the trust to the trust. Update your beneficiaries on your (bank, investment, retirement) accounts to the trust. Work with your attorney and financial adviser to determine what other assets will be assigned to the trust.

Wait! Your homework isn't done yet. Check off everything you've completed:

☐ I've filled out or updated my beneficiary forms. Date:

☐ I've made a guardianship plan for my minor children and/or a special-needs family member. Date:

☐ I've drafted and executed my will. Date:

☐ I've drafted and executed my living will and durable power of attorney. Date:

☐ I've drafted and executed my long-term-care plan. Date:

☐ I've set up and executed a living trust (if necessary). Date:

As you make progress in getting all the above forms finalized, be sure to get two originals of each. Collect them and keep one in a secure place away from home like a safe-deposit box and another in a safe place at home. Again, my recommendation is to purchase a fireproof bag and keep it somewhere where you know your people can find it. If you have a financial planner/adviser, you can also provide them with copies and alert your family as to who should be contacted in the event that something happens to you.

The Leave a Legacy Review

You've learned how to actively plan for what will happen to your estate (cash, real estate, jewelry, and other assets) after you die. This is important no matter the size of your bank account and portfolio, and some parts of your estate plan should be established once you turn twenty-five, or earlier if you have kids or own property.

100% FINANCIALLY WHOLE

You've done it: You are 100% made whole! Your commitment to yourself and to elevating your life through financial wholeness is my inspiration.

If you've worked your way through this workbook, you have a budget, savings, a debt and credit plan, ideas for ways to make more money, a refined investment strategy, adequate insurance, a positive net worth, an amazing team, and an estate plan. Honestly, it's so impressive. Keep up the *good* work; you are worth it, and with dedication and discipline, the only limit is the sky. Let's keep soaring together! Connect with me @thebudgetnista everywhere.

Get Tiffany Aliche's foundational text for financial wholeness.

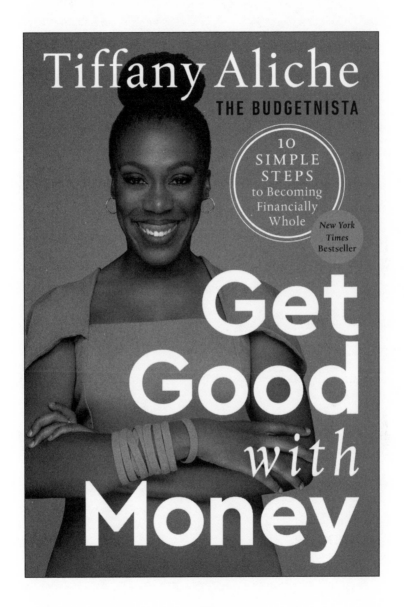

RODALE